A.M.D.

A Classic Path Through
High School
For Exceptional Early Teens

Daniel D. Hickey

AClassicPath.com

Published by AClassicPath.com
First Edition, 2021

Illustrations and Cover Design by Mark Mulligan
Edited by Natasha Reilly-Moynihan

ISBN 978-1-7365961-1-1 hardcover
ISBN 978-1-7365961-0-4 paperback
ISBN 978-1-7365961-2-8 ebook

Library of Congress Cataloguing-in-Publication Data:
Hickey, Daniel D.
A Classic Path Through High School: For Exceptional Early Teens
Library of Congress Control Number: 2021901788
    1- Self-Help Techniques. 2- Interpersonal Relations.

Although this publication is designed to provide accurate information in regard to the subject matter covered, the publisher and the author assume no responsibility for errors, inaccuracies, omissions, or any other inconsistencies herein. This publication is meant as a source of valuable information for the reader, however it is not meant as a replacement for direct expert assistance. If such level of assistance is required, the services of a competent professional should be sought.

For Peter, Brian, and Jack.
Who always make their Dad proud.

Table of Contents:

Introduction:

As you progress from the child your parents raised to the adult whose destiny you will decide, this book is to help you lay the foundation upon which you will build your life. I'm assuming you are a well-adjusted teenager who wants to realize the full potential of their life. Is there such a thing as a well-adjusted teenager? If you are like most teens, you probably don't think you qualify but whoever gave you this book thinks you possess qualities that set you apart from most of your peers. Don't get too excited though, every mother thinks their baby is special. But seriously, someone who loves you wants you to realize your full potential and I'm sure they have told you that this journey of life is not easy. That doesn't mean our time here on earth needs to be drudgery. As you grow into your life, you will find the people you most enjoy being around see life through a positive perspective, the glass half-full to use a common analogy. It is usually not because they haven't faced their share of adversity, it is just that they have a good way of dealing with what life throws at them.

Humans have been facing life's troubles for about 40,000 years, and until recently that often meant life or death. Whether it was dodging dangerous beasts or disease and plagues, most of human history has been a story of strife. Thinking about that makes losing Wi-Fi for a weekend or having to explain a poor grade to your parents seem not so awful. Modern life brings its unique challenges but understanding history helps us overcome the enduring trials of life that people have struggled with through eras and civilizations.

In the following chapters we will experience the story of human history, highlighting some important milestones and advancements, such as writing itself which came about as early as 4000 BC. Some Hindu Scripture and the stories of today's Old Testament were handed down orally for generations before actually being written around 500 BC during an era of great human awakening when people began asking themselves about the meaning of life. That has remained the ultimate question through the history of human civilization up to this day. Most societies have been built around religious beliefs to answer that question.

That is why the first chapter in this book is about God. If you have been raised in a religious home some of it may sound familiar but I hope to present it in a way that shows how philosophy has evolved, and those aspects that have remained constant. Since so much of early human thought was developed under the auspices of the early Christian Church, we will look at the history of philosophy extensively through a religious lens. The Church was also the world's dominant political power for most of its existence and the sole supporter of arts and sciences. Until the last several hundred years, popes were more powerful than any kings or presidents that we could imagine today, so my references to popes and saints are a function of their historical relevance.

The Renaissance in the 15th century was when the value of the written word came to be more widely appreciated by humanity, marking another milestone in human evolution. By this time, Church organizations were teaching upper class people to read and write. A group of Catholic priests called the Jesuits set out in 1540 to educate humanity with lessons dating as far back as the ancient Greeks from two thousand years earlier, such as using reason and logic to question authority. They became so influential that they were actually banished for a few decades before being reinstated hundreds of years ago. In 2013, Pope Francis became the first Jesuit to rise to Catholicism's highest position. The order educates more people today than any other organization. Wherever you are in the world, you are not far from a Jesuit school. Having gone to Jesuit high school and undergraduate college myself, their classical education has a heavy influence on this book.

Once kings began to question the authority of the popes, it would not be long until people began to question their political masters. The Age of Enlightenment in the 18th century was when philosophers began to see humans as individuals with distinct rights. With those rights come responsibilities which are addressed in the second chapter, Country. You will be introduced to pioneering thinkers like Rene Descartes and John Locke and learn how their basic concepts fit into the context of human thought. You will hopefully see how Aristotle's views on friendship from 2,500 years ago are still relevant today. You may never be called to such greatness, but stories about the lives of Abraham Lincoln and Martin Luther King Jr. who overcame extreme adversity and corrected major societal wrongs are meant to inspire you to overcome the adversity that will surely come your way. Chapter 2 also discusses how you fit into your society which generally means your school. Joining groups, developing your talents and letting your actions communicate who you are.

So this is not merely a history book. In Chapter 2 we begin to look at Dr. Daniel Siegel's research into the unique characteristics of the teenage brain. We will look at that more deeply in the following chapters, Sex and Drugs. An objective of those chapters is to show you that much of what happens in those realms has changed little over thousands of years. Teenagers crave novelty and excitement but much of what you might think is new and beyond where others have gone is at least as old as recorded history. Many of the lessons therein are just as old. I want you to learn from the unfortunate role models who fell victim to many of the same challenges that you face today.

Wanting to be popular and succumbing to peer pressure have always been particular challenges for teenagers. We will see common lessons where the easy way that feels good usually doesn't end up feeling too good in the long run. Instead, thinking through the decisions you make will increase the chances that you will be happy with those decisions years later. Your thoughts may not lead you where you wanted, but they will lead you where you belong.

Even though he was a celibate priest, Pope John Paull II thought a lot about sex and the relationships of married couples. His *Theology of the Body* is so groundbreaking that the greatest living philosophers and theologians think he is among only four popes to be considered "Great" and the first in more than 1,000 years. Don't feel intimidated, his concepts are difficult to fully grasp but I hope you understand him enough to realize that he saw the wonders of sex as one of God's greatest gifts to humanity. Therefore not something to be recklessly squandered.

Recent years have witnessed great advancements in research into the human brain. It seems not a few months go by in which another major study builds on the established knowledge we have gained into this enormously important facet of our lives, one that has been largely mysterious to your parents' generation. That accumulating base of knowledge has confirmed Dr. Siegel's research showing the teenage brain to be at a uniquely vulnerable point in our lives. That's why these years can be among the more difficult ones in life. Knowing this should help you manage these natural and temporary weaknesses. The key word being temporary. That doesn't mean life gets easy as soon as you get out of high school. Remember, nobody ever said life was easy. You will read how it isn't even easy for those who look like they're sitting on top of the world. Rock stars like Janis Joplin, Jimi Hendrix and Jim Morrison were able to overcome any burdens from drugs and alcohol in their teenage years but took on deadly habits that killed them by age 27.

A consistent theme through this book is to use these years to build a solid foundation for your life. The habits you form in your youth will likely remain throughout adulthood so make them good habits. You will learn that keeping a sound mind in a sound body was originally articulated in the 1st century and has remained ever since as an integral brick in that solid rock foundation. You do not have to be athletic to keep your body fit. Even those of us not blessed with the bodies we desire can make efforts to keep ourselves in shape and those of us who struggle with grades can still keep our minds sharp. Daniel Boone, the 18th century American pioneer was both. A small man physically with little education, his father once said, "Let the girls do the spelling and Dan will do the shooting." Rather than using freely available fallen timbers, he was smart enough to build his forts with freshly cut trees so they would not catch fire from the Indians' flaming arrows. Chapter 5 is not about rock stars, we cover that previously, it's about the settlement of Kentucky led by Daniel Boone with fortitude and intelligence rarely called for among men.

It is a story about the mutual respect he held with his adversaries, especially the great Shawnee warrior, Tecumseh.

The Shawnees kept a meticulous history so we will get to know Tecumseh from his birth through death. He was a superstar kid who excelled in all the games his friends played and he was universally loved. The solid foundation he built for his life led him to grow into a fierce warrior with morals invulnerable to peer pressure. That made him almost as influential as George Washington was among the white settlers who were increasingly becoming neighbors to the Native Americans in the years preceding the Revolutionary War. It is a more complex story than the common caricature of Europeans stealing land from Native Americans. We will see how people from two of earth's most diverse cultures can share so many commonalities. Good qualities like respect and responsibility passed down from parents to children. Unfortunately also bad characteristics that so often lead to pain and suffering.

I hope the knowledge you gain from the experiences of others will help you build a better life for yourself and avoid some of the pitfalls that have brought down great people. Scattered extensively throughout this book are 14 points that have provided guardrails for people of all faiths, or no religious beliefs, for thousands of years; themes that help people stay on the path they have chosen for their lives. I'm referring to the Seven Deadly Sins and their corresponding Seven Holy Virtues introduced in Chapter 1. These fourteen concepts are classic because they affect all of us, so thinking about how they apply to you will help you avoid the bad ones and embrace the good.

Life is complex and confusing, and not only during adolescence. The stronger you build that foundation of your life, the better you will be able to roll with it all. A book of classic stories would be incomplete without one by the bard himself, William Shakespeare. He has stood the test of time because his subjects are timeless and so is his artful use of the English language. Many clichés, or very common phrases, you will hear as you grow up came from him and surprisingly many come from his play *Hamlet*. It is a story of adolescence meeting adulthood in which a young prince is paralyzed with indecision and confusion. Unlike Daniel Boone and Tecumseh, Hamlet is unable to roll with the troubles life has thrown at him and at the risk of spoiling the ending, everyone winds up dead.

Not to end on a bad note, I conclude the book with the biggest influence on my life when I was your age, The Beatles. Their catalogue of lyrics cover so much of the human experience so I wrap everything up with reflections on how I found solace in their songs through life's confusion and hardship. Decades later I still do.

As you can see, the chapter titles provide a loose structure to explore issues that are important to the adolescent experience. The stories are classic because they address the essence of who we all are. After reading this book, you will be better prepared to construct your life to make your mark on history as you realize your individual talents and potential. Will it be a mark of beauty or a blemish? That answer will be determined by one of my dominant themes, self-knowledge. Throughout the book I will ask you to pause and think about a question, such as:

THINK: How well do you know yourself?

Self-knowledge has been at the heart of human thought for as long as there has been the written word. Clear self-knowledge will direct you towards your strengths and away from your weaknesses. The potential you reach in life will be defined by how much you make the world a better place which will be determined by how well you know and develop your unique strengths and characteristics. Reading this book will nurture that development for you.

I hope you enjoy the stories and learn from them. The chapters are long so take breaks at the section headers, but it is best to read the book in order. Don't be intimidated by words or concepts you don't understand, either take a break and look them up or just read on. This book seeks to broaden many of your horizons, including your vocabulary. As with life in general, you learn when you don't realize it.

Now let's open up our minds for an adventure in reason and logic with Socrates and the advent of philosophy as we dive into Chapter One.

Chapter 1: God

Oh God said to Abraham, "Kill me a son"
Abe says, "Man, you must be puttin' me on"
God say, "No." Abe say, "What?"
God say, "You can do what you want Abe, but
The next time you see me comin' you better run"
Well Abe says, "Where do you want this killin' done?"
God says, "Out on Highway 61"

-Bob Dylan

Bob Dylan captures the absurdity of one of the oldest stories of God, written around 500 BC in or around modern day Israel. The God that made a covenant with Abraham, saying that if he agreed to sacrifice his beloved son Isaac, Abraham would become the leader of a great nation with more descendants than stars in the sky. At God's direction, Abraham built an alter for the sacrifice but before he "took the knife to slay his son"[1] the loving God rewarded him for his loyalty with a ram to substitute for Isaac. It is one of the early religious stories making the point that our decisions and actions have consequences that determine our destiny. Indeed, Abraham became the forefather of three major religions, Judaism, Christianity and Islam.

The story appears in the book of Genesis, written at the beginning of a great worldwide intellectual awakening when humans began to question the world around us and our place in it. Across the Mediterranean Sea, the ancient Greeks had a polytheistic belief in an assortment of gods exerting control over various facets of life on earth. For example, Poseidon was the god of the seas, who punished Odysseus for blinding his one-eyed son the Cyclops with storms and peril on his return from the Trojan War. Aphrodite the goddess of love, frequently got in trouble with her father Zeus, the father of all the gods, for interfering in the affections of mortals. Greek Mythology provides a rich heritage of tales of love and triumph but also common human weaknesses that together form the human condition. Unfortunately, the weaknesses often prevail.

Hundreds of years later, the dominant force on earth was the Roman Empire whose leaders considered themselves gods. People had little control over their destinies then, aside from staying on the right side of Caesar's Centurions. While recognizing their emperors as gods, Romans adopted the polytheistic tradition of the Greeks they conquered. Like the Greek gods, the Latin tradition is rich with lessons about the trials of life and how living virtuously is more difficult in the short term but pays rewards over time. It is a common theme through most religions through the millennia as well as the New Age philosophies of modern times. You will see how other common characteristics also recur throughout various faiths.

Socrates Knew That He Knew Nothing

Although not the first philosopher, Socrates was the first to gain a wide following. Born around 450 BC, he became famous teaching that the way to gain knowledge is through living a virtuous life in search of what is good, which he saw as truth. Socrates wrapped virtue, goodness and truth all together in a single concept. He used logic and reason to question authority as generations of philosophers have continued to do in the 2,500 years since. Socrates did not simply accept the conventional wisdom that the elites of his day were better people than everyone else, and that got him into trouble. His use of logic and reason was so powerful that his lessons resounded despite never committing anything to writing. He would simply sit with his students and convey his wisdom orally. Recording it all for posterity was mostly left to his student Plato who went on to teach Aristotle. Both philosophers continued Socrates' quest for truth and the answer to the ultimate question of why we exist.

Most of what we know about Socrates comes from Plato's writings. In addition to that admirable legacy, Plato could be considered the father of geometry due to his belief that truth can be found in shapes and forms that exist in nature and beyond. Recognizing these forms and how they interact with us is his path to truth. Plato focused on the metaphysical, those things beyond our sensory perception. Only intelligent and enlightened people could recognize these shapes and forms which is why Plato thought society would be best governed by philosophers.

His student Aristotle was more down to earth. Less concerned with the metaphysical, he concentrated on the physical world around us. He saw truth in how our senses perceive the reality around us, those things we see, hear and touch. As one of humanity's earliest scientists, he wrote it all down for future scientists to develop further. For example, his species classifications still form the basis of today's zoology. Not solely focused on earth, he spent much of his time pondering the cosmos. Aristotle is widely credited for determining that the earth is round after noticing that ships sailing beyond the horizon disappeared from the hull first and top of the mast last.

Although incorrect, Aristotle's theory of a geocentric universe, revolving around the earth, formed the basis of science for almost two thousand years. It was intuitive to believe that the universe revolved around the earth because we all see things as revolving around us. This is an early lesson that even the smartest among us can be wrong sometimes, so don't worry if you ever find yourself looking foolish. Aristotle founded his Lyceum school which together with Plato's Academy comprised the School of Athens. They created the educational tradition of which high school is the modern descendant.

Socrates taught his students to ask penetrating questions in a search for the truth which he found through a process of eliminating false theories. When his friend asked the Oracle of Delphi "Is anyone wiser than Socrates?" the answer was "no human is wiser."[2] Delphi was the mountaintop site of a temple dedicated to Apollo, the Greek god of truth and prophecy. It's kind of funny that ancient societies would group those two concepts together; before science, religious prophets were the arbiters of truth. Within the temple sat the Oracle, a priest or priestess who would interpret sounds from the earth as wisdom and truth. Modern science attributes the sounds to probable natural gas springs in the mountain. Socrates humbly tried to disprove the Oracle's assertion but found the elites of his day all lacking in knowledge but thinking they knew much. He concluded that he was wiser than all the politicians, poets and artisans, "because I do not fancy I know what I do not know."[3]

That self-knowledge gave Socrates the confidence to teach the youth of Athens the way to virtue, goodness and knowledge. A common tool was to use stories such as the Allegory of the Cave described in Plato's *Republic* and which I will summarize as follows (try to get past the absurdity and follow the details). Prisoners in a cave have been chained to a wall since birth seeing nothing but shadows on an opposing wall cast by hidden people sitting behind them. The prisoners identify the repetitive shadows and status adheres to the ones who can predict their order. When one of the prisoners is released out of the cave, the light is initially blinding but eventually he can see the real world all around him. Socrates explains that when the man went back into the cave, his eyes needed time to adjust and the other prisoners were better at identifying the shadows still familiar to them. Although the freed prisoner gained true knowledge, the other prisoners mocked him because leaving the cave made him worse at their game, which to them is truth. The other prisoners did not want to be released.

There is a lot in that parable. You can see how truth can be disguised and even blinding when you are confronted with it unexpectedly. It says that what all your peers see as truth may not in fact be true. Notice how the group didn't recognize truth and preferred imprisonment to freedom. It says that it can be uncomfortable to be confronted with truth. It also says you will know truth when you see it and be better for recognizing it. Remember that Socrates conflated truth and goodness as the same

THINK: Which part of Socrates' Allegory of the
Cave resonates most with you?

concept. Just because everyone else thinks something is true, that doesn't make it true, or good.

Philosophers have spent the 2,500 years since Socrates told the story discussing all that it might mean. The politicians, poets and other elites of those days thought it meant Socrates was calling them ignorant. Plato described him as a "gadfly," the first such use of the term previously used to describe insects that fly around and sting the rears of horses. Wanting to get rid of him, the elites of Athens prosecuted Socrates for corrupting the minds of the youth. He used logic in his defense pointing out that the Oracle of Delphi said he is the wisest among men so it was his duty to share his knowledge to make a better society, like the prisoner who is obligated to tell his former captives of the knowledge he gained outside the cave. Unfortunately the jury resembled the other prisoners and rejected his defense; Socrates was sentenced to death by drinking poisonous hemlock.

Confucius Says

Around the same time that Socrates was teaching virtue to the Greek youth, on the other side of the Eurasian continent, Confucius was wandering the kingdoms that comprise today's China also teaching about our control over our own destinies through the decisions we make and the actions we take. The truth in his lessons made Confucius as important to Asian culture as Socrates is to Western civilization. He had to wander because the elites of Asia were not welcoming of his teachings that often cast them in unflattering terms. Perhaps you notice that in ancient Greece and Asia, two very distinct cultures, the smartest minds saw the elites as lacking. That too follows consistently through history so don't despair that so many of today's politicians are also lacking, that's always been true.

Like Socrates, Confucius' greatest impact came after his death when students compiled his lessons to preserve for future generations. You can read his brief *Analects* freely at any library or on the internet. Pertaining to your high school years, you can read number 15 in chapter 2 stating *"If you study but don't reflect you'll be lost. If you reflect but don't study you'll get into trouble."* It is a message urging diligence and balance. Don't get too lost in your books and fail to see the world around you, and at the same time don't be a dreamer who never really learns. Confucius even echoes Socrates when he says *"To know when you know something, and to know when you don't know, that's knowledge."* Self-knowledge and improvement are dominant themes for Confucius just like we see in western civilization. He expands on the concept when he says *"The craftsman who wishes to do his work well must first sharpen his tools."* It is not enough to have the tools and the knowledge to use them. Your skills must be practiced to stay sharp. You may have already realized this from playing sports or music or other activities that get more enjoyable as you practice more. Repeating boring steps may not be fun but overcoming challenges and playing well are. Of course, if you want to play well, you have to do the tedious practice. Perhaps Confucius' most famous analect is a precursor to the Golden Rule so familiar in western civilization, it is commonly called the Silver Rule since it is told from the negative perspective. When asked if there is a single saying for one to practice their entire life, Confucius responded *"That would be reciprocity: That which you do not desire, do not do to others."*

Socrates and Confucius were not so focused on an all-powerful god who would decide our eternal fate. Instead they taught about seeking virtue among humanity for reasons rooted here on earth. Socrates sought social justice while Confucius sought social harmony. Both saw an ethical life as the means to reach those ends.

Between Europe and China sits India, where in this same classical era of great human awakening, Siddhartha Gautama became Buddha which means "the awakened one." Born a prince, he gave up a life of material wealth for one of prayer and meditation. Doing so, he found the path to true enlightenment through a "Middle Way" between self-indulgence and self-mortification. Buddhism also avoids any focus on an all-powerful god but lays out ways of life that enable one to avoid the suffering caused by the evil of this world. Like most religions, the path to wisdom traverses through ethical acts but Buddhism adds deep concentration or meditation. Meditation is when you focus your thoughts completely and totally on the single concept you are meditating about and purge any other thoughts from your mind. Or you could meditate on all the thoughts traveling through your consciousness. You might meditate about your breathing or the sounds of nature where you are sitting or a problem you are struggling with. It could be a deep state of prayer. For many people, meditation is a way to find yourself by searching deeply within yourself.

Buddhism also goes further than other classical philosophies by delving into the concept of reincarnation. Buddhists believe the status you attain in your next life is determined by the way you live your current life. That means if you don't want to come back as a cockroach in your next life you better treat people nicely in this one. Your destiny is determined by karma, the moral law of cause and effect. Karma acts as seeds that come to fruition throughout this life and determine our place in the next. The best way to build positive karma is by studying the Buddha's teachings together with other Buddhists in monastic communities. Leading such a virtuous life will also offset negative karma. You don't have to shave your head and become a monk though, any good thoughts and actions build good karma while bad deeds or intentions generate bad karma. It's not just your actions that determine your destiny but thoughts too, so keep them positive.

Karma also figures prominently in Hinduism whose billion adherents today are more than any other religion except Christianity and Islam. Like Socrates' allegories, Hindu Scripture uses metaphorical meanings to teach the ways to earn positive karma by leading an ethical life. They include accounts of the origin of the world, hymns praising a variety of gods, and prayers for life. The Hindu Scriptures are among humanity's oldest written texts produced between 1500 and 1200 BC.

Originally it was considered a synthesis of the cultures and traditions of a region in northern India, of which Confucianism and Buddhism are major contributors. To those belief systems, Hinduism adds the reading of Scripture and worship of a god or gods but unlike other religions, it leaves any particular practices or rituals to the individual. There is no centralized Hindu authority, like popes or bishops, but there are sages and gurus who help individuals practice their faith in regional, local or personal ways. Pilgrimages are made to common holy sites and daily prayers and purification rituals are common Hindu practices. Cows are sacred in India so if you have a hamburger it won't be made with beef. Several reasons include their gentle nature, usefulness in working the fields and the milk and butter that they provide. A Big Mac in India is made with lamb meat.

For Hindus, the ultimate goal in life is to reach nirvana which is defined in different ways. To some it means full self-knowledge through perfect unselfishness; or it can mean a union with God. Nirvana is defined ultimately as detachment from the desires of this world and perfect mental peace. Hinduism and other ancient faiths and philosophies marked the beginning of humans questioning the purpose of our existence and the religions that followed continue in that search for an answer to life's ultimate question.

Sons of Abraham

When God spared Abraham's son Isaac on the mountain in today's Jerusalem, He promised that Abraham's descendants would found a great nation, and around 1000 BC, Isaac's descendant David prevailed in a battle with the mighty Goliath and went on to found the nation of Israel. Comprised of twelve related tribes of Middle Eastern nomads, they all followed a set of laws that were given to Moses by God on the nearby Mount Sinai.

Known since as the Ten Commandments, the laws have become ubiquitous throughout western civilization, even appearing on the edifice of the Supreme Court of the United States. The first four Commandments relate to loyalty and devotion to God. Family bonds are kept strong by honoring our parents and not committing adultery. The importance of community is stressed in the prohibitions on stealing, killing and telling lies. Finally, we keep our souls sound by not coveting our neighbors' spouses or property. Following these and other laws through the centuries had brought freedom from slavery under the Egyptian Pharos and brought Moses' people to their Promised Land. However, that history is also rife with examples where disobeying God's law brought hardship and strife. David committed adultery and lost a son but he repented and gained God's forgiveness. Archeological evidence confirms Jerusalem's repeated sackings which Scripture attributes to disobeying God's laws. Kind of like generating bad karma and paying a price for it. Beyond the Ten Commandments, Jewish ethics address concepts such as truth, justice, peace, compassion, humility and respect that are found through the various books of what is commonly referred to as the Old Testament.

The most important Jewish holy days comprise Passover, which commemorates the exodus from Egypt and freedom from slavery. Celebrated for the week after the first full moon in April, it begins with a ritual Seder meal including unleavened bread signifying that Moses' people did not have time for the bread to rise when they escaped bondage. The Jewish New Year, or Rosh Hashanah, comes in the fall and is a happy occasion for reflection and resolution for the upcoming year. The reflection continues nine days later with Yom Kippur, a day of fasting and repentance as atonement for the mistakes of the past year. The Jewish tradition is strongly focused on self-knowledge, repenting for your shortcomings and resolving to make the most out of your strengths.

Chanukah commemorates the dedication of the Second Temple in Jerusalem, around 200 BC, after it was sacked and defiled by forces of the Greek King Antiochus IV. Jewish fighters prevailed against the outsiders but when they dedicated the Temple anew they couldn't light the menorah, a candelabra of nine lights, because all their holy oil had been destroyed by the invaders. They found one flask sealed with the signet ring of the High Priest and the miracle occurred when the one-day supply of oil lasted for the entire eight days it took to make a fresh supply. The eight-day holiday commemorates God's blessing of their victory over Antiochus IV.

The Jewish faith holds that God rewards those who keep his commandments and punishes those that transgress them and on a final judgment day will raise those He favors from the dead. In addition to observing religious holidays, the Jewish people seek God's grace by following rituals of cleanliness and purity such as keeping kosher diets and engaging in daily prayer. The rituals have the added benefit of building good habits that lead to an ethical life.

The Jewish Carpenter

Although living under the dominion of the Roman Empire, the Jewish elders known as the Pharisees were the local authorities in Jerusalem at the time of Jesus Christ's birth 2,020 years ago. Mary and Joseph, both descendants in the line of David, were fulfilling their duties as citizens of Rome by travelling to Joseph's ancestral town of Bethlehem to be counted in Caesar's census. A lot of other people were too, so the inns were all full when their baby came, necessitating the humble manger to be the birthplace of the Savior to a third of humanity. By the time he reached twelve years old, Jesus was teaching Scripture to the Pharisees, the high priests, who were amazed at his knowledge of their holy texts. At some point, we all think we are smarter than our teachers but in this case Jesus actually was.

Jesus never showed arrogance, only love. He rejected the common justice of an eye for an eye saying instead to turn the other cheek if someone strikes you. When his fellow Jews asked

Jesus which is the greatest commandment, He said first to love the Lord our God with all your heart and second to love your neighbor as yourself. All Christian laws have these two at their core. Notice how Jesus states loving yourself is as important as loving your neighbor.

THINK: What does it mean to love yourself and your neighbor?

The influence of Socrates reappears when Jesus uses stories, or parables, to teach lessons on how to live the perfect life. The Good Samaritan is the hero of the parable about a beaten man, robbed and left for dead on the side of a road. While others crossed the road to avoid the victim, a passerby from Samaria stopped, helped and cared for him; even though he did not know the victim. The parable is a call to service, to see beyond ourselves and love our neighbors. Since the good man was from far away Samaria, Jesus defines our neighbors very widely as our fellow man.

When the Pharisees brought a woman caught in the act of adultery to be stoned, they confronted Jesus to agree that the law should be upheld. Instead Jesus said that he who is without sin should cast the first stone. The lesson is that self-reflection and not being judgmental are integral parts of leading an ethical life. Surely we can all think of things we regret doing ourselves and are glad we got away without a mob throwing rocks at us. The Pharisees didn't like Jesus showing such compassion to those who have violated God's law so He answered them with parables like the Prodigal Son.

It is the story of a rich man with two sons, one of whom requested his inheritance early. The father agreed and the young son went on to waste all his money by living extravagantly. Then a famine hit and the son realized that his father's servants lived better than him. He returned home to beg forgiveness and ask to be hired as a servant. But before he could ask, his father ordered a huge feast and the finest robes to adorn his son who was lost but

was now found. The other son obviously wasn't too pleased to see such a celebration as his loyalty and devotion had never been so rewarded. The father reminded the older son that he has already inherited all that the father has, so he should be happy for that and also happy for his brother's redemption.

This marks a very significant development in the history of God and religion. Jesus tells us that God forgives our transgressions and celebrates our contrition. Even if we have not led an ethical and good life, we can still gain salvation and eternal peace if we repent and ask for forgiveness. He is a God that will not only liberate us from the suffering of this world but will also liberate us from our own sinful ways. And it is never too late!

It is a powerful enough message that Christianity quickly spread across the western world, but some of the popes forgot Jesus exhortation to "render unto Caesar the things that are Caesar's and unto God the things that are God's."[4] The Catholic popes in the Middle Ages became the most powerful rulers on the planet. As Rome was forced to fight more wars to protect a swelling empire, the emperors were becoming weaker and their terms in office shorter as others jockeyed for power. Political power shifted to the Church and many of the popes resembled politicians loving their power more than God. They were not all bad however as three of the popes considered "Great" reigned in the 5th through 9th centuries.

St. Gregory the Great, the patron saint of students and teachers, was pope from 590-604 taking the humble title "Servant of the Servants of God." He was revered around the world for his kindness and generosity. Raised in a wealthy family, he began a tradition of giving by turning over most of his own wealth and property to the Church. Other wealthy families did the same and Gregory had meticulous procedures for distributing the wealth to the poor. During times of famine, he directed the Church's significant landholdings to produce food for rich and poor who were starving. He revitalized a wayward church becoming famous for his sermons that taught virtue to his congregations and missionary skills to his bishops. It was through his ministry that

The 7 Deadly Sins and 7 Holy Virtues		
Anger	-	Patience
Greed	-	Charity
Laziness	-	Diligence
Pride	-	Humility
Lust	-	Chastity
Envy	-	Kindness
Gluttony	-	Temperance

Christianity spread throughout northern Europe, making the continent Catholic. One of Gregory's legacies is the formalization of the seven deadly sins to supplement the Ten Commandments.

Although they were developed before his reign as pope, his theology said that *anger, greed, laziness, pride, lust, envy* and *gluttony* are the origin of other sin. Each is a form of selfishness that prevents us from living an ethical life. Contrary to each are the seven holy virtues of *patience, charity, diligence, humility, chastity, kindness* and *temperance* to protect against the temptation from the deadly sins. All fourteen are present in all of us and determine how we treat others and how we regulate our own behavior.

Anger can manifest in violence towards others and countless self-destructive ways like drug abuse and suicide. On the other hand, **patience** leads to peace and forgiveness and results in a more stable community.

Greed refers to an unquenchable desire for material possessions that can only lead to emptiness and dissatisfaction. It is better to receive joy from being **charitable** towards others, practicing the virtue that encompasses neighborly love and general self-sacrifice. By learning to do without the things we want, we come to know those things that we truly need. Have you ever given something to someone without wanting anything in return and found that the joy in watching them receive your gift was the greatest gift in return? If so, you have achieved a high level on Aristotle's hierarchy of friendships that we will explore in the next chapter.

Laziness is something that afflicts most of us in some form. In the sinful sense, its meaning is broadened to include not realizing our talents and gifts, so wasting time would be included. It is much better to use your extensive teenage energy to be **diligent** in the tasks that will strengthen the foundation you are building for your life.

The ancient Greeks considered **pride** to be the deadliest of sins as it was the source of others. Literature throughout the centuries has consistently identified it as paramount among human weaknesses. The dramatic change that occurs in our teenage years makes us naturally self-centered and especially susceptible to pride. As we become more knowledgeable and physically adept, it is natural and good to be happy with ourselves which makes it more important to show **humility** and be respectful of others. It doesn't mean thinking less of ourselves, it means knowing ourselves and being open to improvement.

Lust refers to intense sexual desires that make us objectify others, sometimes those we do not know but often those we care about and love. Rather than seeing the person, we merely focus on their body. **Chasity** means deferring sexual activity and prevents the dangerous behavior that often follows. It lets us learn how to love the person and not the body. We will look at that further in Chapter 3.

Envy is unhealthy in the way that greed and lust are. It leads us to make poor decisions based not on truth but negative emotions that can cause harm to those around us and ourselves. True **kindness** will make us happy for the good fortune of others and lead to other virtues like charity and humility that often form the base of strong friendships.

Gluttony refers to over consumption of food or drink but can be broadened to over-indulgence in general. Its consequences are obvious, from short term discomfort to disease and death.

Temperance, meaning self-control and restraint, is a quality that will come in handy when we try to get in shape or when times get lean which happens to most people at some point on the great journey of life.

Becoming aware of how the deadly sins and the holy virtues relate to you will help you become knowledgeable of yourself and your own strengths and weaknesses. That self-knowledge will make the foundation you are building for your life stronger. It doesn't matter if you are religious or not, they are classic points because they affect all of us in varying degrees.

> **THINK: Which of the deadly sins and holy virtues are most applicable to you?**

Islam

It was just after Gregory's reign as pope that a young descendant of Abraham from a merchant family on the Arabian Peninsula was praying in a mountain cave when the Angel Gabriel came to him with a message about the Lord his Creator. The appearances continued over a period of years with continued messages of how to lead a virtuous and ethical life. The messages were relayed orally and recorded by his followers who saw him the same way more than a billion and a half people do today, as the Last Prophet of God in a long line preceding Abraham, including Moses, Jesus and others but ending with Mohammed.

The written verses comprise the Quran, the Muslim Holy Scripture. Without separating the realms of Caesar and God, the Quran is not only a set of personal laws but also the legalistic framework for society at large, a political governing philosophy as well as a theology. In addition to the written word, the record of the prophet's life is called the Sunnah reflecting his words, actions and personal characteristics. Along with the Quran, they are considered the sources of Islamic principles and values.

Those values include the responsibility that man has to worship his creator who will have final judgment over all of us. The worship includes frequent daily prayers asking for forgiveness from sins and help for those in need. Charity towards the needy and regular donations to the poor are principal requirements of Muslims. In addition to virtues to be pursued, the Quran lays out explicit crimes to be avoided with the goal of pleasing God and gaining entry into heaven. Islam sees education as an important way to learn how to distinguish right from wrong; it is at young adulthood that Muslims begin to fully participate in the traditions and responsibilities of their religion.

Muslims focus intensely on their faith during the month of Ramadan when they fast in atonement for their sins and ask for God's forgiveness. The fast lasts each day from dawn until sunset from one crescent moon to the next. It is a time of increased devotion to God and spiritual reflection. In addition to fasting, Muslims also refrain from other less than virtuous behavior and speech during Ramadan. The fasting is meant to build self-discipline and self-control and to develop empathy for those less fortunate. Like other religions, the rituals form good habits that lead to good behavior and keep one on a righteous path. While Muslim traditions are as unique as Christian, Jewish and ancient faith traditions, you are probably noticing similarities in these and other religions where we are called to surmount our shortcomings and develop our strengths.

When Mohammed went out across the Arabian Peninsula to preach his message, he met hostility similar to the prophets that preceded him. The other tribal leaders did not appreciate the charismatic effect he was having on the youth who joined his growing band of followers. As his philosophy was a political order as much as a religious one, it eventually prevailed across the region and spread wider over subsequent centuries to where 1.6 billion Muslims make it the world's second largest religion today.

Philosophy Becomes Enlightened

Wars fought in the name of God engulfed the next several centuries and human civilization stagnated for a long period that became known as the Dark Ages. Several centuries marked by plagues and political disruption ended with the 15th century Renaissance, when art and science began to once again flourish under giants such as Michelangelo, da Vinci and Galileo. All of western civilization's writing was done in Latin and Greek until the multitudes of earth's oral vocabularies took a great leap forward with Johannes Gutenberg's invention of the printing press in 1439. After that, people were able to share words and thoughts more freely so more people learned to read and write in their native languages. Literature developed into mainstream entertainment and science began to be shared more widely. With everyone expressing themselves, a blossoming of human thought led to cracks in the political order as protest became possible. The most significant example was in 1517 when a monk named Martin Luther pinned a list of 95 grievances he had with the corrupt Church officials on the door of his church in Wittenberg Germany. It resulted in the Great Schism in Christianity and the establishment of various Protestant faiths.

In this next great era of human awakening, classical teaching from Socrates onward came back into prominence as culture began to focus on human nature and the individual's place in society. Science quickly advanced to where it increasingly conflicted with Church teachings. In the most famous case, Galileo, the father of modern science, developed an improved telescope that enabled him to see shadows on the planets that disproved Aristotle's geocentric theory of the universe. Disproving the foundation of science for 2,000 years and contradicting religious authorities, Galileo knew his discovery would cause controversy and get him in trouble. He published his work anyway because it was the truth. Scientific truth was more important to Galileo than his own comfort, so he followed his conscience and did what he believed was right. As he expected, the Pope banished him to house arrest until his death for proving that the earth revolved around the sun, contradicting the Biblical Psalms which state the earth does not move.

Galileo died at home in January 1642 and later that year Isaac Newton began what would become a hugely consequential life. Walking in his mother's garden one day, he wondered why an apple falls from its tree directly to the ground in a straight line. Something so basic and common captured his imagination and he had to determine why. His studies resulted in his theory of gravity which became just a part of his *Principles of Mathematics* and provides the foundation of modern physics. You never know when your curiosity may lead you to great places as it did with Newton's apple. Now the world had a new authority on the nature of things. Science and reason were becoming more in conflict with religious dictums.

After the Renaissance spawned a new society confident enough to question its masters, the Age of Enlightenment saw philosophy increasingly separate humans from any divine aspect or function. Living during Galileo's time, Rene Descartes said "I think therefore I am." Up until this point in human development, knowledge derived from sensory perception. His example was that fire is hot and can melt wax. Melted wax changes its form but perception alone is not enough to fully understand the reality. Reason is required to deduce that the hot flame melts the wax. Therefore, Descartes said that knowledge is not based simply on sensory perception but also reason and thinking. Thus was born a philosophy that said much of what humans take on faith from religious authorities is wrong, such as the "knowledge" that the cosmos revolved around the earth. Faith was increasingly seen as conflicting with reason, a concept we still hear about in the 21st century. However, Descartes described himself as a devout Catholic and said his enlightenments only meant that there is more that God is revealing to us than mankind currently perceived. Maybe he just said that so the pope wouldn't banish him.

Dominant philosophies of the 17th and 18th centuries focused on the individual and his place in society rather than God's role in our lives. It was thought that an ethical life could be led without the influence of a specious god. 19th century Existentialists like Friedrich Nietzsche kept their focus on the world in which we live and not some metaphysical concept that may or may not exist. He saw God as a fiction created by those who cannot face the difficulties of this world. For Nietzsche, the goal in life was to become an Ubermensch, or Superman, who overcomes adversity to master his destiny. A character from one of his books famously says "From life's school of war: what does not kill me makes me stronger."[5] He said morality is fine for the masses but exceptional people should not be ashamed of their uniqueness but rather flourish in a "will to power." It's an appealing concept as we all like to see ourselves as strong and powerful and we don't like to be constrained by morality and rules. But as the ancient Greeks taught, pride is the deadliest of sins. Nietzsche's philosophy fed the concept of a master race that appealed so much to Adolf Hitler a generation later and gave us the worst disaster in history, World War II and the death of millions.

The horrors of the 20th century gave rise to various New Age philosophies that generally focus on the individual while reaffirming some form of deity as an overpowering influence in our lives. Many borrow from Asian philosophies and those found in Hinduism. Some emanate from science fiction literature and tell of other beings from outer space waiting to reveal true wisdom to us. A common theme across New Age philosophies is the holistic self in which mind, body and spirit all work together to affect our wellbeing. These philosophies shun traditional routes to wellness which are mostly limited to the physical world in which medicine reacts with illness to heal the body, or psychotherapy treats mental problems. New Age adherents say these lack the integral spiritual component where some deity is involved with our wellbeing, it could be the sun or Mother Nature or even the god of Abraham. Of course, our actions play a large role in that wellbeing or lack thereof.

Faith and Reason

"Know Yourself" was carved on the Oracle's temple at Delphi in ancient Greece and ever since then self-knowledge has been at the heart of all the philosophies and religions that followed. We cannot improve ourselves and reach our potential unless we know our shortcomings. Self-reflection reveals the strengths we should be grateful for and the weaknesses we need to overcome. The paradox that also runs through most of these philosophies is that self-knowledge is achieved through selfless acts. By removing ourselves from ourselves we can truly see ourselves. Do something nice for someone else and you will know what I mean.

All the various religions and philosophies also agree that as individuals alone we are insignificant to the world around us. It is how we bring our unique attributes into that world that determines our destiny, and that is within our own power. None say it is easy and all point to evil as present in this world in some form. Self-knowledge helps us overcome the evil that prevents us from leading an ethical and fulfilling life.

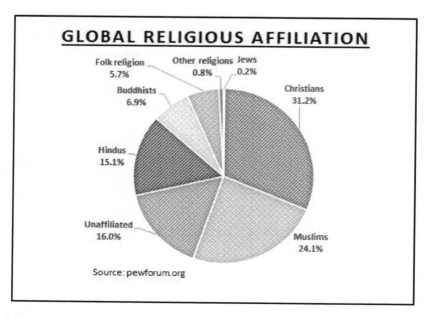

The nearby chart was produced with data from the Pew Research Center through regular studies they conduct on religious affiliation around the world.[6] It shows the percentage of the world population that follows each religion. You can see that includes all but about 16% of humanity who are unaffiliated with any religion. Since no religion accounts for more than half and they all hold different truths, it follows that most of humanity is following a faith based at least partially on false truths. It must be the similarities we have seen that matter. All of those people try to follow an ethical lifestyle that leads to the rewards they believe will follow. The percentages have been generally consistent through generations so there must be some reason why all these people through all of modern times have found meaning in their religions. While we can't know if following religious precepts will help us in the next life, we know how all these religious practices help to build good habits. Your own logic and reason can tell you how that will help you through this life. After all, six billion people can't all be wrong.

However, the loudest voices in modern society say they are wrong. They claim to be more concerned with science than theology even though the latter is built on the former. They say they believe in Darwin and not Adam & Eve even though Darwin said his theory of evolution does not explain humanity and the Catholic Church recognizes the Creation story as allegorical. It may have taken more than seven days to create the world we know but it is proven scientific truth that the cosmos, earth and life thereon were created in the same order as presented in the book of Genesis. Intuitive thinking of ancient times would have seen the earth being created before the cosmos. Whoever wrote the Creation story found truth by thinking outside the box and whatever began to evolve into today's humanity must have been created by someone or something. Understanding how science and religion interact will help you decide what you believe.

St. Thomas Aquinas

Some of the best thinking on that topic was by St. Thomas Aquinas in the 13th century. He posited a series of Socratic like arguments to reach the conclusion supporting Aristotle's view of an "unmoved mover" or God who must have set all of existence into motion. St. Thomas Aquinas saw faith and reason as complementary. He said theology based on Scripture confirms the science we observe in nature, such as the cosmos being created before the earth. A far greater leap of faith is to believe that the harmonious existence of everything making up the world and cosmos is all a lucky accident.

True faith must be challenged. If faith is not combined with reason it really isn't faith, it is simply believing what someone else told you. St. Thomas Aquinas discerned truth by listening to all points of view. Considering false points of view and finding them to be false, was his way to find truth.

Conversely, those who think reason cannot be combined with faith are inhibited by rejecting a powerful force accepted through history as integral to the search for truth. If one rejects the existence of God, they will turn a blind eye to any evidence of God's presence, such as miracles, the complex harmony of nature, or the simplicity of a baby's smile. As Socrates might have asked, can you really use reason to answer the questions of our own existence if you reject the possibility of God's existence and His role in it?

THINK: What do you believe?

The greatest scientist of modern times was Albert Einstein whose theory of relativity explains the physical world as involving the concept of time. Finding everything except the something that created it all, Einstein also accepted the unmoved mover as the creator of the orderly harmony of all that exists. Early in his career he said "strenuous intellectual work and the study of God's Nature are the angels that will lead me through all the troubles of this life with consolation, strength, and uncompromising rigor." Einstein did not believe in a God active in our daily lives like most religious people do, but one responsible for creation. However, even without the incentive of redemption, he saw the ethical life of strenuous work providing the strength and consolation to deal with the inevitable troubles that we all face.

You are at the age where most religious traditions accept you as an adult. Maybe you have been recently Confirmed, or celebrated your Bar Mitzvah, or just began fasting during Ramadan. That means you believe the teachings of your religion because you have thought them through and see them as the truth. The religious observances you may have begun to practice are meant to build the kind of ethical lifestyle that will reveal knowledge and truth to you. They are meant to establish the good habits that will keep you on a virtuous path. They are also to remind you of something bigger than yourself. Even if not religious, we all need guardrails in our lives and until now your parents have set them with hopes of putting you on an ethical path. Becoming an adult means you set those guardrails for yourself. That is just one reason why it is so important to know yourself.

The Catholic Church's fourth great pope, St. John Paul the Great, frequently used the phrase "Be not afraid!" It is a message that appears in various forms frequently through Scripture. It is what Jesus told his disciples who faced crucifixion like he did for not recognizing Caesar as their god. The great advancements of human history occurred when people overcame their fears to push the limits of knowledge. Galileo knew the pope would not accept his discovery but he overcame his fears of imprisonment and published his work anyway. Fear is one of the most difficult emotions to overcome because it is always easier to recline into our comfort zone than to face the object of our fear.

As you build the foundation of your life, be not afraid! Push beyond your comfort zone as you lead an ethical life in an unending search for truth. Set personal guardrails to keep your life in line with the holy virtues and away from the deadly sins. Discover yourself by serving others and interacting with those around you. If you lead an ethical life, your conscience will keep the right choices apparent, but they are usually not the easy ones. The right choices though are the ones that lead to the greatest rewards in the long journey of your life. If you don't know the ethical answer to a difficult dilemma, contemplate on it for a while. Meditate over it. Pray about it.

Chapter 2: Country

And so, my fellow Americans: ask not what your country can do for you, ask what you can do for your country.

-    John F. Kennedy

President John F. Kennedy appealed to our ethical sensibilities in his inaugural address on January 20, 1961, as he took over governance of the most powerful nation since ancient Rome. The American colossus, founded on the importance of the individual, had recently saved the world from tyranny in World War II, thanks largely to citizens putting their individuality aside in pursuit of a common cause. The victorious soldiers came home to the ladies who had kept the US economy running and together they created the baby boom generation of 75 million Americans born from 1945 to 1965. Speaking particularly to that new generation benefiting most from America's rising dominance in the world, Kennedy asked everyone to contribute to American exceptionalism in our own unique way by realizing our individual talents. Little did he know the world was on the cusp of a cultural revolution driven by the "Me Generation" celebrating their personal individuality. Although an assassin's bullet kept him from witnessing it, they achieved Kennedy's goal to put a man on the moon while changing the world like it had never been changed before. It marked a new era where individuals realizing their unique personal talents built today's American economy enjoying history's highest standard of living. It's been a long journey from the way the world used to be.

The concept of country and governance has changed quite a bit since the long line of Caesars were the most powerful rulers on earth. Over the next several centuries, emperors like them ceded power to popes who ceded to kings and princes. Europe and Asia had each become a hodgepodge of small kingdoms that would go to war with their neighbors and then marry off sons and daughters to make peace and expand their borders. In this period of political instability at the end of the 15th century, a government bureaucrat from a well-connected family in Florence, Italy wrote a book describing the "new prince" who needs to maintain political stability among the governed to protect his own position of authority. Even a dictator who rules by force has to remain in the good graces of the governed. Niccolo Machiavelli's *The Prince* written in the early 1500's came to define the phrase "the ends justify the means" to excuse unethical political acts if they assist the ruler in enacting an ethical agenda. Rulers usually claim their agendas to be ethical. In Machiavelli's view, virtue for the political leader is whatever strengthens his hold on power. This Machiavellian philosophy will inevitably collide with the Enlightenment movement where human individualism will assert itself as an opposing force.

Articulating that opposing force was John Locke and his views on natural rights bestowed by our creator which challenged royals claiming divine rights to their power. He wrote in the late 1600's that our minds gain knowledge as a combination of sensory perception and personal reflection. You can see the evolution of human thought where Locke synthesizes the viewpoints of Aristotle and Descartes. Moving it a step further, he believed human nature to be characterized by reason and tolerance but that it is also within our nature to become selfish. Locke saw government as a mechanism for civil society to resolve conflicts among all its self-interested individuals. While acknowledging the necessity of an administrative power, he thought that personal property should be free of government ownership or control because it is the accumulation of the value of our own personal labor. That's a very important concept in human evolution, instead of working on behalf of a king or lord, Locke saw property as the fruits of an individual's own labor.

Great Britain became the next world superpower by employing this philosophy which gave birth to a flourishing industrial economy based not on agriculture, like most economies until that time, but manufacturing and trade. Individuals realizing their own unique talents devised ways to make and market new products for sale around the world. More than a century later, Karl Marx criticized the concept of personal property, writing that a great class struggle would inevitably break down all class distinctions and eliminate personal property. Marx called for government to take control of everything for the benefit of everyone. Enlightened leaders like those that Plato envisioned would ensure the equitable distribution of goods and services. Vladimir Lenin put the theory into practice beginning with Russia's October Revolution of 1917 and the resulting Soviet Union enjoyed superpower status for most of the 20th century. The totalitarian state however was not strong enough to withstand the power of human individualism that drove the European and American economies. The Soviet rulers failed at Machiavelli's primary concern, they lost the consent of the governed. Their government dissolved before the 20th century came to a close.

While Marx's theories have never met success, Locke's influence was instrumental to a band of radical intellectuals fighting for independence from Great Britain at the height of her power. Generations before his birth, a wave of Locke's ancestors left England for the new world. Word back from William Bradford's 1620 settlement at Plymouth Plantation told of a land of freedom and plenty even though Bradford's journal tells a story of hardship and strife before those rewards came to fruition. Starvation nearly wiped out the colony in the first winter as the communal methods of farming failed to produce enough food. The Pilgrims had no incentive to work hard because everyone shared in the fruits of their labors equally, so low standards prevailed and production suffered. The solution was to give each colonist his own parcel of land to farm as he wished. Production blossomed as individual colonists grew different crops to trade amongst themselves and the initial American economy was born.

Of course, it wouldn't have happened without the friendship of the native "Indians" who taught them how to farm the local land.

By 1776, the American economy had grown over 150 years to be one of the most dynamic on earth as the new world attracted the entrepreneurial minded from around the old world. America was the place where individuals could pursue life and happiness as they saw fit. The land was also rich in forests and livestock whose lumber and furs could be sold back in the old world. Those strong enough to withstand the long ocean journey came to various colonies that appealed to different kinds of people. Tradesmen and manufacturers came to northern colonies whose flowing rivers and waterfalls powered the mills that produced all sorts of finished products. Farmers were more attracted to the warmer climates and fertile landscapes of the southern colonies. The colonists chose political representatives who met in Philadelphia and designated Thomas Jefferson of Virginia to draft their declaration of independence from the British Empire. That was a monumental decision in world history, no colony had ever tried to break free from an empire before. Nobody could be confident of success and everyone that participated knew the King's punishment would be death.

Inspired by John Locke's philosophy on the sanctity of the individual, Jefferson wrote of the "self-evident" truths that "all men are created equal" and "endowed by their creator with certain unalienable rights." Unalienable means those rights belong to the individual and cannot be taken away by any political authority. The colonists declared it to be the "Right of the People" to alter, abolish or institute a new government. This was truly a revolutionary concept that had never been attempted before. Although democracy was invented in ancient Greece, they practiced a more modest form. More than two centuries after Jefferson's Declaration, representative democracy dominates the world order today.

John Locke and the other Enlightenment thinkers who inspired the American Revolution saw our natural freedom and rights as carrying great responsibility too. That's what President Kennedy meant when he asked us to think about what we can do for our country. It only works if society is focused on improvement, when most people want to do their part to make the world a better place. Like the philosophers and scientists who hone their thoughts to withstand scrutiny, the tradesmen who build products that improve our lives, the officials and soldiers who protect us, or the entertainers who bring a little more joy into life. They all practice their special talents for the benefit of us all.

> **THINK: How might you make the world a better place?**

At your point in life, your education is your greatest responsibility so that you can learn how you might best contribute to society. Concerning education, Locke said "I think I may say that of all the men we meet with, nine parts of ten are what they are, good or evil, useful or not, by their education."[7] This goes all the way back to Plato and Aristotle teaching about the ethical path in life being a search for knowledge and truth. For as long as recorded history, it has been known that living ethically and following your conscience will reveal the knowledge and truth that lead to success and happiness.

A Foundation for Greatness

The colonists who signed the Declaration of Independence knew that King George would take it as an act of war against his throne. They had already been fighting the Revolutionary War for about a year since Congress had formed the Continental Army and appointed George Washington of Virginia as its commander in chief. In Washington they found a leader who had proven himself to be diligent, humble and patient for what promised to be a long and brutal war. Even though he lacked a formal education and religious background, Washington was undoubtedly familiar with the Deadly Sins and Holy Virtues. After his father's death, the 11 year old was unable to afford the education of his typical upper middle class peers. He had family friends who tutored him and a school run by Anglican clergy gave him the equivalent of an elementary school education. In addition to losing his father, several siblings died at young ages including his older brother who had been his surrogate father. Contracting smallpox while caring for his ailing brother wasn't enough to kill the future leader and in fact inoculated him against the disease that would kill many of his soldiers in the Revolutionary War. Like Nietzsche wrote decades later, that which did not kill George Washington, made him stronger (but the analogy ends there.)

Out of such adversity came Washington's greatness but it wasn't automatic. He had strict rules that he set for himself, published today as *Washington's Rules of Civility & Decent Behavior*. It is a collection of 110 rules of behavior that he wrote out by hand. The rules were originally assembled by Jesuits who had been missionaries in North America but were few and far between by the time of Washington's childhood. Some of the rules are not relevant today, like eating outside or not, but those dealing with respecting your elders and people in authority are truly timeless. The first rule states: "Every Action done in Company, ought to be with Some Sign of Respect, to those that are Present." That means to always be considerate of those around you. It's a great rule to begin with because if you get in the habit of thinking of others, so many other good habits will follow and you will find yourself on a great path in life. Subsequent rules cover aspects of speech, manners and behavior. Number 4 says not to hum or tap your fingers or feet in the presence of others. Do you have a tendency to do things like that? Isn't it interesting that people in those days did too? You might not realize how annoying it can be to others. Number 44 helped Washington be a great leader, it says not to blame someone who tries hard but does not succeed. The Revolutionary War was marked by numerous setbacks for the colonists and if the General had strongly admonished his troops for every failure, he would not have been able to maintain morale among his army through all the hardship they faced.

Washington's patience and kindness were enough to keep the army assembled through the long winters when some of his soldiers didn't even have shoes and other basic equipment. Kind of like today's politicians, the early US Congress consistently failed to authorize sufficient payment for the troops, so most were fighting without pay. Washington's leadership instilled hope in the troops that their cause was just and therefore victory would come. His ability to recruit an army willing to fight under such harsh circumstances might be attributable to rule number 56 which states: "Associate yourself with Men of good Quality if you Esteem your own Reputation; for 'is better to be alone than in bad Company." Think about that when you choose your friends. Are you hanging out with a good crowd? Of course with most classics, a modern reading broadens "Men" to include everyone.

Some of Washington's rules address avoiding gossip and minding your own business. Regarding business, he implores to only take assignments that you can fulfill, and then fulfill them well. The rules end with number 109: "Let your recreations be manful not sinful;" and finally number 110: "Labor to keep alive in your breast that little spark of celestial fire called conscience." Washington recognized our conscience as a gift of celestial fire, meaning coming from God. He knew how important it is to listen to your conscience, it will usually keep you on the right path.

Setting these guardrails for himself formed the foundation for George Washington to fully realize his potential and become one of the greatest people who ever lived. He was the only colonial military leader in world history who ever defeated an empire. His lack of a strong religious upbringing didn't restrain him from embracing precepts that came from religious authorities. The values he held dear, articulated in the rules he chose to live by, make him the example for all leaders to emulate.

> **THINK: Have you set any rules for yourself to live by?**

Actions Speak Louder Than Words

Four score and seven years (in other words, 87 years) after the colonists declared their independence, President Abraham Lincoln delivered the Gettysburg Address at the Civil War battlefield for which it is named. Grade school students were often required to memorize the 271 words said to comprise the greatest speech ever given. In it, Lincoln honored those who gave their lives so the nation "shall have a new birth of freedom—and that government of the people, by the people, for the people, shall not perish from the earth." He recognized how revolutionary and fragile the concept still was almost a century after being adopted. That new birth of freedom was especially poignant for the African Americans who had lived in slavery until Lincoln's Emancipation Proclamation freed them. Slavery was America's original sin and the country had come to a point where it could no longer be countenanced. Lincoln is among the greatest Presidents of the United States but nobody would have expected it from the lanky laborer in his adolescent years who became a hard-working prairie lawyer before he became a politician.

In the great Lincoln - Douglas debates, the future president would assail his competitor for a US Senate seat for supporting the institution of slavery which was counter to the nation's founding principle, stated in the Declaration of Independence, that all men were created equal. He lost that Senate race but so impressed the country with his powerful eloquence that he eventually was elected to lead the country through its darkest years. Aside from being America's bloodiest war, some basic liberties like freedom of speech and the right to not be unjustly detained were suspended during the Civil War. Historians have called him Machiavellian for some of the questionable means by which Lincoln achieved his ends, but nobody debates the importance of preserving the Union and ending slavery. It was only after the stain of slavery was washed from the fabric of America that the country became the true beacon of freedom to the world.

Lincoln's greatness was not sought but thrust upon him by his peers. His eloquence came from the truth of his message backed by the weight of his deeds. Until Lincoln's Emancipation Proclamation, Jefferson's pronouncement that all men were created equal did not fully ring true. Lincoln's Proclamation finished what Jefferson's Declaration began. If you asked any of Lincoln's teenage friends if they thought he would become president someday, they would probably have said he is diligent and kind but such an odd looking and poor fellow could never reach such a pinnacle. However, 150 years later, no leader has reached a higher status.

THINK: Which of your friends might become a great success?

At the core of Lincoln's greatness was not his eloquence but doing what is right. Born poor in a one room log cabin, his life was marked by extreme pain and suffering, early and often. He was hired out as a laborer by his oppressive father who kept all his earnings. That could explain his empathy for the slaves. His mother died when he was nine and his sister died a few years later. When he was a young man, his first true love died of typhoid fever and his next love didn't work out. Although he eventually married in a state of doubt and anxiety, he and his wife Mary had five sons who he cherished by all accounts. Losing four of them to untimely deaths exacerbated this poor man's endless suffering. Can you imagine having to endure such hardship?

It would be easy for any person facing far less to give up all hope and doubt that anything good could ever come of their life. Lincoln never wavered. Hardship made his casual faith in God grow stronger. He educated himself all the way up to a law degree and traveled the state of Illinois working hard for every client. He saw elective office as a way to help the downtrodden before he saw it as a way to correct the country's original sin. His faith in the rightness of saving the Union gave him perseverance through the deadliest war in American history.

Lincoln never looked for the easy choice, only the right choice, and that made him great. It wasn't easy to prosecute the Civil War and save the Union, and he met vehement opposition to the Machiavellian decisions he made. His Emancipation Proclamation was politically unpopular when he issued it but was ultimately ratified by Congress and the states with the 13th Amendment to the Constitution that bans slavery. Some say his second inaugural address is his best speech, delivered after the Civil War and 42 days before he was assassinated, in which he delivered the conciliatory message: "With malice toward none; with charity for all; with firmness in the right, as God gives us to see the right, let us strive on to finish the work we are in." As great as America was, he saw it as still unfinished work.

Truth to Power from a Birmingham Jail

A century later, African Americans were free but still not equal under the laws of the segregated southern states that treated them as second-class citizens. They couldn't sit at lunch counters with white Americans or drink out of the same water fountains. They had to sit in the back of busses and let whites sit in the front. The injustice called upon another great man to rally his nation to see what was wrong and make it right. On Easter Sunday 1963, Rev. Martin Luther King Jr. wrote his letter from the Birmingham City Jail answering his critics who said he was pushing too hard for change. He had been leading demonstrations across the southern states for 8 years since a black woman named Rosa Parks refused to give up her seat on a bus to a white woman. She said she was "tired of giving in." The defiant act cost Rosa Parks her job as a seamstress at a local department store. She became active in the civil rights movement and became a friend of King who was a new Baptist minister in her town of Montgomery, Alabama.

King's father was also a Baptist minister who was very strict with his three children, regularly whipping Martin until he was 15 years old. The boy grew up suffering from depression either from that treatment or because any friendships he would strike up with white kids would be snuffed out in the racist environment of the 1950s southern states and their "Jim Crow" laws. His grandmother died when he was 12 years old and he blamed himself because he was away from home at a parade without permission. Perhaps ashamed about his self-perceived failure, he was so stricken by grief that he jumped out of a second floor window. Fortunately, his suicide attempt failed and the episode got him thinking about the afterlife. Martin's maturing adolescent brain was naturally beginning to question his beliefs and at age 13 he told his Sunday school class that he didn't believe Jesus rose from the dead. By age 18 he had rebuilt his faith from scratch and decided to enter the seminary to become a Baptist minister preaching the Good News of Jesus' Resurrection. That's a lesson not to be too sure of your views today, they may change tomorrow.

Martin Luther King Jr. had experienced too much systemic injustice and knew he couldn't change society all by himself. Joining the civil rights movement was the best way to devote his life to serving others. He got arrested leading a boycott in Birmingham Alabama on Easter Sunday. Easter happened to be the second busiest shopping season of the year so his organization determined it was an opportune time to lead a demonstration against the white merchants and their "humiliating racial signs."

King had a four step process to his non-violent campaign:
- Ascertaining facts
- Engaging in negotiation
- Self-purification
- Boycott

He didn't simply get mad and react, that would have played into the white majority's views that the blacks only wanted to cause trouble. Instead, he thought about and devised the best way to overcome the injustice. The facts were clear for all to see and his letter eloquently explains just a handful. He wrote of "forever fighting a degenerating sense of 'nobodyness'" among the reasons "why we find it difficult to wait." Think about that powerful word "nobodyness." It means being someone whose thoughts and aspirations carry no bearing in society. Can you imagine if your hopes and dreams didn't matter? King's organization agreed to delay their demonstration "as weeks and months unfolded" but the promised negotiations never came. The self-purification occurred when King and his followers asked themselves if they were prepared to "accept the blows without retaliating" and "endure the ordeals of jail." That is where they ended up for demonstrating without a permit even though the permit was denied, which he explains was a violation of his free speech rights.

THINK: What does "nobodyness" mean to you?

His 7,000 word letter (almost as long as this chapter) expresses frustration with "the white moderate who is more devoted to order than to justice" and he laments "the appalling silence of the good people." It was easy for good people to be silent, nobody ever wants trouble. King called out people who considered themselves to be good, telling them their silence is appalling. He sought to create tension among those moderates like Socrates created tension among the ancient Greeks "so that individuals could rise from the bondage of myths and half-truths." It was a common belief at the time that blacks were intellectually inferior to whites. They certainly didn't have the education and opportunities that whites had. The myth of inferiority was akin to the prisoners in Socrates' cave who believed their false perception of truth.

Rev. King tells his critics that one has a moral responsibility to obey *just* laws but also a moral responsibility to disobey *unjust* laws. He quotes St. Augustine that "an unjust law is no law at all,"

and continues with St. Thomas Aquinas arguing "Any law that uplifts human personality is just. Any law that degrades human personality is unjust. All segregation statutes are unjust because segregation distorts the soul and damages the personality." He explains that justice must respect the individual and segregation obviously prevents certain individuals from realizing their God given talents and potential. He references a legal maxim dating back hundreds, if not thousands, of years that "justice too long delayed is justice denied."

Martin Luther King Jr. was initially disappointed in being called an extremist but came to favor the term. "Was not Jesus an extremist in love? – 'Love your enemies'... Was not Abraham Lincoln an extremist? – 'This nation cannot survive half slave and half free.' Was not Thomas Jefferson an extremist? – 'We hold these truths to be self-evident, that all men are created equal.'" The question is "will we be extremists for hate, or will we be extremists for love?" Despite the horrid injustice of the times, King was optimistic saying the "goal of America is freedom" and he saw his people as an integral part of America since "before the Pilgrims landed at Plymouth." Turning Machiavelli on his head, he writes "nonviolence demands that the means we use must be as pure as the ends we seek."

Like Socrates, he willingly accepted the consequences for his actions in order to arouse the conscience of the community. He did indeed arouse the conscience of the community when a few months later hundreds of thousands of people of all races gathered under Lincoln's memorial in Washington, DC to hear King's speech about having a dream that one day his four children will not be judged by the color of their skin but by the content of their character. Dr. King finished that classic speech longing to sing "Free at last! Free at last! Thank God Almighty, we are free at last!" The demonstration and speech won him the Noble Peace Prize but five years later on April 4, 1968, Dr. Martin Luther King Jr. was also assassinated. He did not die in vain, fifty years later the fire of his spirit burned brightly when his children were able to vote for the first African American President of the United States.

Behind the Mask

For this part of your life, in many respects your school is your country. Your school places responsibilities on you like government does for adults. It is the society in which you participate in social functions and groups. These years are a time when you will discover those characteristics that set you apart from your classmates but also place you within a certain social ecosystem. When I was in high school there were jocks, nerds, arts people, and certainly others I can't remember anymore. In any school at any time there are all kinds of circles of friends who hang out together and at least one of them should appeal to you. Maybe they dress alike or use similar language, consciously or not, which shape their personas. They comprise a group of friends which grows organically with likeminded people. Sometimes it can take a while to find your friends but if nobody appeals to you, maybe you need to know yourself a little better. Think about how the seven sins and virtues apply to you.

These are the years when you will develop your persona. It is a word you have heard and probably understand but maybe more so when you know its derivation. Webster's dictionary defines *persona* as *"the way you behave, talk, etc., with other people that causes them to see you as a particular kind of person: the image or personality that a person presents to other people."* In Latin, *persona* means a theatrical mask. Maybe the definitions are not too different.

We all present ourselves as we want others to see us and we all hide certain aspects of our personalities. We don't want to expose our weaknesses and we don't want others to think we are intimidated by them, even when we are. Our personas are a subtle form of communication where we tell others about ourselves, what interests us, what we do for fun. Others see us by the language we use, the clothes we wear and the hobbies we pursue.

Finding our place in society is easier when we are true to ourselves and others; when we keep our personas as close to reality as we can. If you falsely present yourself as a karate master, you will inevitably be shown to be a fool. If you are a teenage karate master, that would be an important part of your persona.

As you look around your school you will see how someone's language tells a lot about their persona. Someone who speaks as taught will be perceived as a better student than someone who speaks in street slang. Different groups will use terms that come to identify them and individuals will use language to define themselves too. Someone who uses foul language will occupy a different place in society than someone who speaks respectfully, and the two people will probably hang out with different groups. The topics you speak about also define your persona. Some people are more interested in sports while others prefer entertainment. Some seek to speak above their level to make themselves sound smart while others speak in a way to make themselves sound cool.

> **THINK: What is your persona?**

Communicating our persona is not only defined by what we say but more importantly by what we do. The eloquent words of Lincoln and MLK are remembered because they were from the heart, true, and backed by righteous actions. Although we may never be called to such greatness, we should still live our lives truthfully and righteously. Do we join the crowd in making fun of the hardships of others or show kindness like the stranger from Samaria and help even those we don't know? Are we overly proud of our strengths and oblivious to our weaknesses? Do we know ourselves enough that our personas resemble our true personalities rather than our aspirations? The answers will determine how others see us regardless of the mask we wear. That will play a role in how we ultimately find our place in society. How we dress and style ourselves may identify us as members of a particular circle of friends but outward indicators like that are merely superfluous to our true personalities. Think about the people you know and how they are genuine or phony, or maybe some of each.

Confucius says *when you see a worthy, think of becoming equal to him; when you see an unworthy person, survey yourself within.* The first part of that analect is an excellent tool for building your persona and your true personality. What makes one *worthy* of emulating? Look for where the seven virtues or other admirable qualities are present in such a person. Are they patient and kind? Diligent and humble? Emulate those characteristics that you admire about the person and they will probably become your friend.

The second part helps to keep your persona closely aligned with your true personality. Of course you will avoid people you view as unworthy of your friendship, but Confucius' advice is to "survey yourself within." That means to look at what makes the person unworthy and make sure you do not hold those characteristics yourself. If so, you will either gain respect for those you previously saw as unworthy or change that characteristic about yourself. Self-knowledge must precede self-improvement.

Aristotle's Friends

Even though he was wrong about the cosmos, like so much of what Aristotle wrote 2,500 years ago, his thoughts on friendship are just as relevant today. In *Nicomachean Ethics,* he describes friendship as a hierarchy of three types. All friendships require us to give pleasure to our friends and are sustained by reciprocal good will; we are friends because we enjoy having a good time together. That may be the only basis for a particular friendship in which case it is the most common type. Think about a group with whom you play games or hang out with regularly. Even a wider group of many people that come together at larger social functions would contain many of these kinds of friends.

On the next level are less common friendships of utility where benefits derive from being friends. Think about a friend who invites you to exciting events or being able to invite a friend to something that they otherwise wouldn't be able to attend. Like giving that gift of joy when we covered charity in the last chapter. Maybe being a friend with someone gets you invited to fun parties or the cool lunch group. A good player on your team who helps you win games could be such a friend. Aristotle says these friendships have stronger bonds than friendships of simple pleasure and will be more durable. You will share a sense of loyalty with these friends.

The highest level of friendship is the rarest. It is reached when we share the same values as our friend and wish them good will only for their sake. These are friendships that take time to develop. Aristotle quotes the proverb saying true friends cannot know one another "till they have eaten the requisite quantity of salt together." He's talking about sharing the spice of life; all the fun and excitement but also the hardship and struggles. These types of friendships will survive when any utility is withdrawn and even when there's no pleasure to be found. When your problems are so overwhelming that you can't have any pleasure, you will know who your best friends are. The cliché *a friend in need is a friend indeed* goes almost as far back as Aristotle.

Digital friends are another story. Some are the Aristotelian kind and have moved away but stay in touch digitally. This is as friendly as Thomas Jefferson and John Adams writing letters to each other in their old age, Aristotle would probably rank it highly. Digital media is a blessing that enables us to maintain such rare friendships even when facing the challenge of distance. That could refer to a friend who moves across the country, or one who has been grounded by their parents, or all of your friends sheltering at home during a pandemic.

Instantaneous digital communication lets us share our joys with those we love no matter where they are but also carries clear risk. It may not be obvious to you yet, but your high school years will include many words and deeds you will want to take back. Digitizing them makes them permanent. When you are interviewing for a job in the future, you don't want your prospective employer to ask you about that embarrassing online photo or comment. This is a challenge your parents didn't have to confront. I could say and do all sorts of stupid things when I was younger and it is all forgotten now (I hope). Older generations didn't have to worry about someone snapping an embarrassing picture and posting it online, but today we all do. Murphy's Law says that your worst digitized moments will arise at the most inconvenient time in your future, so as with everything in life, be careful. Our digital world also has other more subtle but pernicious risks.

Friends that are only from the digital realm do not meet a qualitative definition of friendship. You may gain pleasure by playing video games with someone on the other side of the world, and you may even get to know that person to some extent. You may get to know people digitally who share a common interest and help each other develop related skills. Such relationships certainly provide pleasure and utility but typically do not develop to where you share values with your counterpart and wish them good will only for their sake. That is because they are friendships that go no deeper than one's persona and we have no way of knowing the actual personality behind it. We usually do not even use our real names online. (That definitely does not ensure your anonymity.) There is nothing necessarily wrong with such relationships, they just fail to provide the attributes of friendship that we all need. We build friendships up to the higher levels when we get to know our friends better. Only seeing what they choose to show online prevents us from gaining that knowledge. We may know the persona but not the person. The way to really get to know someone is to look through the window into their soul, their eyes. You can't do that online, not even with Facetime and Zoom.

When we spend time with our friends online, we need to be aware of George Washington's first rule of civility to always be considerate of those in our presence. Clicking away on your device with such a friend while ignoring one in your presence sends a signal that the friend on the device is more important. Have you ever tried to have a conversation with someone who is more concerned with the person they are texting with? Maybe we want to signal to others how popular we are so we look busy communicating with all our friends. Or maybe we are frantically hoping one of these superficial friendships will develop into a real one. Behaving like this doesn't build friendships, it erodes the bonds we have with those in real life and spoils the opportunity to strengthen those bonds. We end up portraying a popular persona that contradicts an empty feeling of loneliness inside. There is an accumulating body of science that links excessive time spent on social media with higher levels of depression. Too many people have plenty of online friends but nobody at Aristotle's higher levels because they are constantly ignoring the natural friends around them.

> **THINK: Do you spend more time with friends digitally or in real life?**

The true friends that you spend time with know you and help you develop your personality by encouraging your better qualities and helping you overcome your weaknesses. A true friend will point out particular skills or talents that you may not realize you possess, or suggest groups or activities that you didn't think would appeal to you. A true friend will give you constructive criticism, not to bring you down but to make you self-aware. It's nice to get plenty of digital *likes* but the opinions of those who know you best should carry the most weight. If you spend all your time buried in your phone, who will be that true friend who can really help you become a better person?

Your Individual Talents

Your true friends will play a role in determining your place in society by helping you develop the talents that will be most consequential to your life. We all have some quality that sets us apart from others, maybe athletic or artistic ability, maybe an intellectual or business capacity, or maybe leadership or charitable qualities. The progress of humanity comes from people recognizing their talents and developing those special abilities to make the world a better place. That's what President Kennedy asked us to ask ourselves. It can be especially difficult for high school students to discover their talents because they are usually not proficient at anything yet, but hidden talents can emerge in unexpected ways. Menial labor at an entry level job can reveal an aptitude to organize or innovate. Serving customers can reveal interpersonal abilities. Your studies will reveal subjects that capture your interest more than others. Leading an ethical life will reveal your talents like it reveals other truths. If you are patient, diligent and humble, you will find that special talent that defines you as an individual. Once you think you have found your special talent, it is your responsibility to develop it to your fullest extent for the benefit of society. It won't only benefit others, you will find your efforts lead to bigger and better experiences and a rich and full life.

Discovering your talents is part of knowing yourself and essential to realizing your potential. Your potential is defined by those characteristics you hold that can contribute most to society. Approaching life with a mindset of serving others will encourage you to develop those characteristics of your personality that can help others the most. Maybe you can inform or entertain, build bridges or scientific theories. Maybe you are destined to work in nature, industry, politics, medicine, finance, law or sales. Your goal is to make the world a better place, for you and everyone else. Realizing and developing your talents is how you achieve that goal. If you are like most high school students and doubt you are talented at anything, just get involved in what interests you. Every school offers a wide array of extracurricular activities. Joining groups and engaging in activities will naturally place you within your ideal societal ecosystem. At the very least, you will enjoy the search. Every philosopher asks what our reason for existence is, while the answer is within our own grasp. Discovering your unique, individual talent will answer that question for you.

Grades are Money

Unlike the adult world, the currency of status in high school is not money but grades. It may seem like prowess on the athletic field or stage brings status; or good looks and busy social calendars. If you look beyond all the superficial aspects of popularity however, you will probably find that those whose friendship you value the most take their studies seriously and truly spend their days learning in an ongoing search for knowledge. We naturally gravitate towards people like that because we naturally gravitate to that which is good.

There are plenty of smart people who are not necessarily good students. If that describes you, then good grades mean better than before. Maybe you are not an A student but getting Bs instead of Cs confirms that your search for knowledge has been fulfilling and that you are preparing to become a valuable member of society. Good grades in geometry reflect knowledge that can help you build a set of steps when you get your own home and also help you understand Plato's philosophy about forms in nature. Understanding language arts like poetry and literature will teach you about the power of the written word and how it reflects the constancy of human nature. Shakespeare may be difficult to read but experiencing how his characters are similar to people you know will teach you about dealing with all kinds of people. An understanding of science and technology could set you up to solve any of the problems that continue to vex humanity. If you want to be a great doctor that cures a pandemic, you better enjoy chemistry in high school. Knowledge of history will alert you to when it may be repeating itself so that you can better understand what is happening in the world around you. That will be useful when you have to navigate the real world. Understanding how philosophers have viewed the world will help you understand how you fit into it. You will study a wide array of subjects in high school which will teach you how to become a functional member of society, the more you master those subjects the more you will master your life.

Beyond your grades, having a better understanding of the world will enable you to enjoy it more. Tending a garden will help you understand how energy progresses from the sun to our food to our own bodies. Observing animals will reveal how life fits with nature. Joining groups that get out into nature will help you understand how mankind has always fit into the amazing and beautiful ecosystem that is earth, and its small place in the great cosmos beyond. It will also remind you of our tiny individual places in the world around us, lest we become too proud viewing the world as revolving around ourselves.

Since we naturally gravitate towards the good, we naturally want to share the knowledge we acquire, like Socrates' prisoner going back into the cave. Joining groups is a way to share that knowledge with those that find it most useful. In that way, joining a group is a form of communication in itself. It says you have an interest in a particular game, art form or some other subject and maybe even have knowledge to share. Those with the most knowledge carry influence because they have the most to contribute to the group. The athlete who is most diligent in honing his skills to master his game, while maintaining a respect for his teammates, might be chosen as the team captain. It takes more than just proficiency though. The best chess player will only become the president of the chess club if she is kind and humble enough to earn her colleagues' respect.

This is an area where pride and humility can come in conflict. Especially in our modern society, we are expected to make our virtues known to elevate our status. That's why so many people lie about being virtuous. We are constantly inundated with ads extolling a product's superiority because we all want to buy the best. Likewise, since we want to associate with the best and the brightest, we want others to think that is who we are. It drives us to post achievements on our social media forums and seek leadership positions. There is nothing wrong with that, we should be proud of our hard work. We just need to have enough humility to know that even if we possess an extraordinary talent, it does not make us better than others. No matter how good we may be at something, we can always get better. So rather than stoking our own pride, it's best to remain diligent and constantly improve ourselves. The greatest performers are humble enough to never stop practicing. Since nobody likes a braggart, striking the proper balance between being proud of our accomplishments but humble at the same time is one of life's enduring challenges. That's why the ancient Greeks saw pride as the deadliest of sins. Just being aware of the dichotomy should keep you on the humble path. An honor student bumper sticker on your parents' car is on the safe side.

THINK: What makes you proud?

Those too proud of themselves will lose the admiration of others or even worse, will fall victim to the ancient Greek concept of *hubris* where pride leads to disastrous consequences. An example is the myth of Icarus, the son of Daedalus, an Athenian master craftsman who needed to escape certain death on the island of Crete. The father built two sets of wings for his son and him so they could fly off the island and away to safety. The wings were made of feathers and wax so the father warned his son to follow the path he flies. Too close to the water and the dampness could weaken the feathers and flying too close to the sun could melt the wax. Icarus was enjoying the flight so much that he ignored his father and let his curiosity bring him too close to the sun. Having been too proud to follow directions, the wax melted and he fell to his death in the sea below, still named today the Sea of Icarus.

You will see several examples in the next few years of people riding a wave of popularity only to see them crash for any number of reasons, but usually because their personas were not true. Those who are diligent, charitable and kind, while conducting themselves in a humble way, will likely have truer personas and more solid friendships. They may not be among the most popular early on but they will be by the time you graduate. The class valedictorian will be the best student who also has respect for their classmates and earns their classmates' respect in return.

Your Maturing Brain

A seminal point in your life will come when you get your driver's license, letting you experience more of the responsibilities of being a citizen. Think of the country those great leaders like Washington, Lincoln and MLK have given you, and try to live up to their excellence. You may find our traffic laws to be unjust but be prepared to pay the consequences for disobeying them; and let's hope that's limited to paying a fine and not the far too common consequence that so many teen drivers face. The following chart with 2018 data from the US Centers for Disease Control shows the causes of death among Americans aged 15 through 24. You can see that traffic accidents are the most common cause.[8]

The second leading cause is suicide which could result from deep mental illness but also from the confusion and despair that are common to the adolescent experience. Your body and brain are producing new hormones and neurotransmitters in unfamiliar ways that can make you feel very uncomfortable. Family, friends and mentors or counselors are the best people to help with those kinds of issues but only when those who are suffering let their support network know. Don't be afraid to discuss unpleasant feelings with others. You may find them to be normal or you may get essential advice on dealing with them therapeutically. If you are constantly feeling anxious or depressed, don't be too proud to seek help.

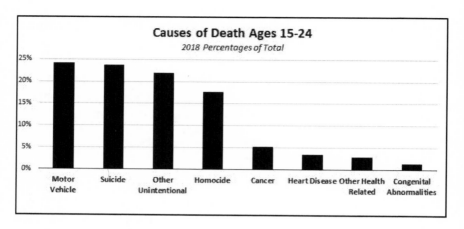

The Other Unintentional bar represents poisonings, drowning and other accidents all of which are preventable as long as we progress carefully along the path of life. Some of the homicides are surely a result of innocent people being in the wrong place at the wrong time but most are related to whom we choose as our friends. When you hang out with the wrong crowd you are likely to end up in the wrong place at the wrong time. Someone reading a book like this wouldn't hang out with such a crowd though, would they? The important message is that over 87% of deaths among this age group are preventable.

Scientists have studied why so many teens face untimely deaths and recent research into the human brain has provided answers to help you understand this important phase of your life. Modern imaging technology has shown that when we are younger our brains grow beyond the amount we need and before adolescence there is a blossoming of the neurons that transmit the information that our brains process. These neurons are brain fibers that grow like a bush. The process matures in our pre-teen years at which point the brain actually begins to prune those areas that are not used,[9] much like one would prune an overgrown bush. Or to use another analogy, it's like pathways being paved over to make highways. Because this is such an active remodeling process during our teenage years, we face different emotional characteristics than at other periods in our lives.

One difference that neurologists have found is that teenage brains weigh reward much more heavily than risk. [10] That explains why you hear stories of teens doing stupid things like jumping from high points or driving as if they were in a video game. Teenage brains focus on the thrill and excitement from such behavior more than the obvious risks of serious injury or death. Knowing this, you need to be especially conscious of the decisions you make and the risks they entail.

My high school drew students from a wide area so many of my new friends were from different towns and counties. That provided a good way for me to learn more about the diverse region in which I lived. This day must have been in the summer after sophomore year because we were driving. Mike brought Neal, Chris and I to the "country club" which was a spot at a reservoir where we were not allowed to swim, making it a perfect swimming hole for thrill seeking teens. On the way to the secret place, there was a bridge spanning part of the lake that Mike told us he had jumped from with other friends. Wanting to experience the thrill, we parked along the side of the road, walked onto the bridge and looked down below. I had taken high jumps before but none this high. It's probably more than thirty feet. Feeling that teenage thrill craving, we all stood on the bridge knowing we couldn't wait long or the police would pass by and see us. Mike explained how we needed to jump in a particular spot to avoid a rock hidden just below the surface. He offered to go first so we could see where to jump.

Yelling and screaming on the way down, he splashed into the water. A few seconds later, he still hadn't come up. Neal, Chris and I were terrified that he hit the rock and we all felt compelled to jump in to rescue him. Except that we were afraid to also hit the rock and by then we weren't sure where his entry spot was anyway. After a little while of a worried discussion, a clearly amused Mike appeared swimming backstroke from under the bridge asking if we were coming in. The bridge wasn't too high for him to hear our conversation and we realized the practical joke that had been played on us, there was no rock beneath the surface. We all jumped in after him looking for retribution. On my way into the water I mistakenly had my arms stretched out and the impact from hitting the water left the undersides of both arms red for hours. It hurt enough to teach me the lesson to keep my arms at my sides whenever we made the jump again.

We went back to the "country club" quite a bit that summer. On one occasion, the police snuck up on us in a motor boat. We all fled, leaving our radio, cooler and clothes behind. The police were calling out to us in the woods saying they had our stuff. We thought it was better to relinquish it all rather than get a summons for swimming in the reservoir. Reflecting on it with what I know now, one of the reasons why we went to the "country club," rather than the real country clubs we could have gone to, was because we got a dopamine surge from the illegality of it. Dopamine is a chemical produced in the brain when we feel these thrills, we will look at it more in the next two chapters. The thrill didn't come from the jump alone but from overcoming the risk of getting caught. If the police captured us that day we would have been in a little trouble but we were all well-adjusted enough to not take stupid risks. It's not as if we were putting our safety or futures in serious danger. We all trusted Mike who knew the bridge was safe to jump from because others had taken him there before.

The thrill craving among teenagers generally peaks around age 15 after which the brain becomes more adept at processing complex scenarios.[11] This period is not necessarily a disability though. Thrill seeking can lead to dangerous behavior but it can also serve a positive purpose. It can expose us to new friends and new experiences. The four of us at the "country club" didn't know each other before high school but we are all still friends decades later with bonds that go back to those thrills we shared in our teenage years. You can't get real life experiences like that by texting with friends. Memories like that only come from real experiences that can't be shared through a screen. Losing all our stuff that day to the police was what Aristotle meant by friends sharing salt together.

It is during adolescence that we are most adept at learning, which makes discovering groups and activities so rewarding. Studying humanity through the ages, anthropologists have found consistency through diverse cultures that adolescents have always desired novelty, excitement and friends.[12] Oftentimes, a new and exciting experience with friends can lead to discovering an innate talent that you possess. If you want to take up a musical instrument or new language, these are the years to do it before you become an old dog resistant to new tricks. Spanning eras and cultures, the tendency for teens to crave novelty and thrills is a genetic characteristic thought to prepare us to leave home and make our lives in an unfamiliar world.[13]

That world will become more familiar when your parents give you the car keys so here are some other facts to store away for your neural transmitters to process when you begin driving. Not only do teens suffer the highest incidence of traffic accidents, the rate increases when friends are in the car or when the driver is speaking on the phone.[14] Speaking on the phone while driving slows your reaction time down to that of a seventy year old, so a good idea is to turn off the phone before you turn on the car. Texting while driving should probably fall under the suicide category, don't fool yourself into thinking you're the only human who can text and drive at the same time. Also not surprisingly, risk of a crash increases with speed so follow the traffic laws, they exist for a reason.

The great leaders through history have shown us that two wrongs do not make a right, but three lefts do. You can always make your way back to a missed turn rather than swerving across lanes. Learning to drive is not as much about the tricky aspects like parallel parking as it is about the everyday habits like observing speed limits and making full stops at stop signs. Driving is a wonderful rite of passage in our lives that broadens our horizons and teaches us to develop good habits and be more responsible. You will even find that you become more selfless and want to run errands for your parents!

You will learn that the best in life is not free when the car needs gas, and you will appreciate it more if you earn the money yourself. You will also learn that machines need maintenance when you need an oil change or have to fix a flat tire. It is all worth it though because most of life is someplace else and you need a car to get there. Even if you are a city slicker without need for a car, try to get your driver's license anyway. Your high school will probably have a driver's education program and you will inevitably come to use your driver's license someday.

Driving lets you see more of our great world and play more of a role in society. Will you be one of those tailgaters always angry at other drivers or will you patiently fit into the flow of traffic? It can be a metaphor for life. We have seen how our behavior can be a more powerful form of communication than what we speak, as important as that is too. Hopefully your good example will make our highways safer for everyone.

THINK: What do you most look forward to doing in your high school years?

Getting out and making the best of the great gift of life is the way to make that life most rewarding to yourself and your community. Whether or not you drive, find ways to get out with friends and participate in group activities. Finding your unique special talents will lead you to groups of friends and the fun and rewarding experiences that will define you as a person. Even when your life doesn't feel like much of a gift, be like Washington, Lincoln and Dr. King who turned adversity into greatness. Overcoming adversity and keeping a clear focus on the truth, gave them all the fortitude to achieve their great objectives. Learn to behave like those you admire and you will find that others emulate you.

When you find your friends doing things that you wouldn't do, or hanging out with a bad crowd, reassess the friendship. It will surely happen in your high school years and you will have to ask yourself if your friend is engaging in adolescent curiosity or truly dangerous behavior. Are they living outside the guardrails you set for yourself? They will want you to also do what they are doing. How high is the bridge they want to jump from? Should you try to correct your friend's behavior, let it pass or let the friendship drift away? These are the questions you will grapple with in the coming years and a true knowledge of yourself will provide the solid foundation from which to answer them.

Knowing your talents or at least knowing what attracts your interest will keep you in an orbit with those who are naturally inclined to be your friends. How you behave and who you decide to associate with is how you communicate your persona. Is it true? Can you see your new friendships developing up to Aristotle's highest level? Engaging in your areas of interest will build your talents and set you up to contribute most to society when you fully enter it in your adult years. Remember, your brain is a work in progress so keep your emotions in check and think twice about the risks and rewards of the actions you take. Most importantly, don't become a statistic. They aren't going to name a sea after you like they did for Icarus.

Chapter 3: Sex

The veriest coward would become an inspired hero, equal to the bravest, at such a time; Love would inspire him.

- Plato, *Symposium*

According to his biographer, Pope John Paul II liked to think about philosophy from the standpoint of Adam in the Garden of Eden. It helped him see the world through a fresh perspective with all the wonder and astonishment that Aristotle believed was the beginning of philosophy.[15] There is nothing more wonderful and astonishing than sex, and philosophers have spent millennia pondering all of its meaning. John Paul pondered Adam's loneliness in the Garden of Eden before Eve was created. He was lonely on a certain level because he was different from all the other animals in that he had rational thought and free will. At the same time, he was obviously also different from God who created him. So man's original state was loneliness, one of the more common states of humanity ever since. However, love came to Adam when God created Eve. Their life together was pure happiness defined by nudity and pleasure enjoying all of God's great gifts, until the serpent tempted them to eat the forbidden apple. After committing this original sin, Adam and Eve both realized they were naked. They were ashamed and covered their genitals with fig leafs.

Since then and through most of time, sex has carried negative connotations as pertaining to our lowest animal instincts while of course being necessary for procreation. Socrates saw it as an obstacle on the path to knowledge and virtue. Plato said the beauties of the body are nothing compared to the beauties of the soul. His quote above relates to a story where the gods were jealous of human love and spitefully split humans in two. Ever since, the state of humanity has been a search for our other halves, our soulmates. Couples who truly fall in love have found their soulmates, that person who fully complements them. Common thought in ancient times, as reflected in literature and other art, was generally like it is now. Those in love know that sexual activity can bring a culmination of their love in a euphoric metaphysical experience. As you are maturing physically, you know that our sexual bodies can also be used for that simple base pleasure that barely separates us from the wider animal kingdom.

Ancient Greek men were well known to enjoy sexual relations with other young men, it was so common that there wasn't even a word for homosexuality in ancient Greece. Art from the preserved ruins in the ancient Roman city of Pompeii shows people engaged in all sorts of sexual acts that could be found on a typical pornographic website today. Prostitution has also been prevalent throughout history earning its moniker as the world's oldest profession. Today as always, sexuality drives emotions that often lead us down an unethical path. Lust and gluttony may bring momentary pleasure but they appear on the list of seven deadly sins for good reason.

Ancient Sex

The Hedonists of ancient times believed that pleasure is the most important intrinsic good. Their philosophy can be traced to a student of Socrates, Aristippus of Cyrene. The Cyrenaics differed from Socrates and Plato in that they preferred bodily pleasures which they considered more simple and intense than intellectual ones. They recognized however that some pleasures can lead to pain so the wise person will control their pleasures and not be enslaved by them. As we will see in the next chapter that is easier said than done and their school of philosophy died out within a century.

Other Hedonist philosophies came and went over the centuries where sex was viewed in a variety of ways. Epicureans ascribed more to the Socratic view that knowledge and virtue were the ultimate pleasure and were attained by abstaining from bodily desires like sex. Living in Greece more than a century after Socrates, Epicurus and his followers saw pleasure as the absence of pain and therefore sought modest and sustainable pleasure. That viewpoint made temperance an important virtue for them. The term is used today to describe someone who enjoys life's sensual pleasures such as fine art and cuisine. The ancient Epicureans saw sex as objectifying the partner which inevitably leads to disappointment. We will see how using those we love to achieve our own personal pleasure persists through cultures and philosophies as one of the conundrums of human sexuality.

When people think of ancient Hedonists today, the image is often that of the Roman Bacchanalia which began as occasional female parties made in homage to Bacchus, the Roman god of wine. Wherever there are ladies drinking lots of wine, men will surely follow. The parties developed into frequent sexual orgies including all social classes and ages that would degenerate into drunken violence. It is another example of sex bringing out the worst in people. The Roman Senate passed legislation in 186 BC banning the cult surrounding the festivals in what might be the first official act in a long history of sexual repression. Despite the legislation, the cult and the Bacchanals lived on for many years.

The Senators were reacting to reports of violence and death at the Bacchanals but there were other reasons to repress promiscuous lifestyles in society. Sex outside of marriage has historically been seen as fostering harmful consequences. The Ten Commandments ordered Moses and the ancient Israelites not to commit adultery or to desire a neighbor's wife because of the social disorder that often followed. Broken families have never been good for society, especially when a cohesive family unit was so important to one's economic wellbeing. Before there were schools, children needed to be taught by their mothers while fathers went out to support the family. Children born and raised without this necessary family support became a burden to society. Promiscuous lifestyles caused other social problems such as sexually transmitted diseases (STDs) which could spread quickly through the public lacking basic health care services. Reasons like these led societies through time and geography to establish laws addressing sexual relations, even if such laws often sprang from bigotry.

Single parent families are normal in our modern society with wide social support mechanisms that provide public healthcare, housing and food. Even with all that, becoming a parent in your teenage years would have an enormous impact on you, and a greater impact on your child. Taking on such a vast responsibility would surrender years of rewarding exploration before you would typically settle down with greater knowledge to enter the parenting phase of your life. Teenage bodies are undergoing extremely active hormone levels making it the easiest time biologically to conceive a child, so you need to be very careful with the decisions you make. It falls on your own logic to ensure your decisions will have a positive impact on your life and the lives of others.

Sexuality binds all of humanity across class and culture, almost everyone experiences it eventually. Looking east from Europe across Asia and into India we find the *Kama Sutra*, probably written around 400 – 300 BC, it is an ancient guide written for the elite class who saw sex as a luxury recreational activity. The book suggests ways for men to attract a lover and all kinds of sexual positions to try out with their wives or their mistresses and prostitutes. More than just sex, it guides its readers on how to maintain power in a relationship and when to commit adultery. Common through most of history is sex as a male dominated activity; it is a history of a man's world after all, until modern times.

Renaissance Woman

After the ancients, most of the history of sexuality is a story of repression by church authorities who so often flaunted their own laws. By the 16th century, women gained new status in

70

Renaissance art and literature. Some of the most beautiful paintings of all time feature not stately men but nude buxom women enjoying libertine lifestyles. Protestant thought in the period increasingly viewed sex within marriage through the lens of marital love rather than procreation alone. It became OK to have sex and enjoy it, as long as you are married. Marriages began to be based more on romantic love rather than family interests. Whether art imitates life or the other way around, women of the era benefited from the emergence of courtly love of the type that appears so often in Renaissance art and literature. Being placed upon a pedestal wasn't all good though, as much of the male dominated culture simultaneously characterized women as voracious sexual beasts who exploit men's primal appetites. It was another way for the authorities to discourage promiscuous lifestyles while keeping women subjugated in society.

The Renaissance era was also when private bedrooms became common, providing privacy for more frequent sexual activity. German and French historians refer to the period as "the age of bastards" resulting from more people having children from multiple partners.[16] It was a minor sexual revolution until the emergence and spread of syphilis swung the societal pendulum back the other way. A new STD to hit Europe, people had little immunity to it as it became particularly virulent. Patients would suffer from open sores, fever, severe headaches and other intense pain and delirium. The disease would infect the brain causing insanity and finally death. Looked at in the grand historical context, it is not surprising that the next major societal trend was Victorian prudishness.

The ethos during the reign of Britain's Queen Victoria in the mid to late 1800s was to hide all expressions of sexuality in order to eliminate the troubling thoughts that often follow. Victorian women did not show any skin other than their faces and hands so as not to tempt men who may come in their contact. Elaborate gowns hid any hints to the shape of the body underneath. Literature was censored of inappropriate material and male and female authors had their work separated on library shelves.

Museums even covered ancient nude statues with strategically placed fig leaves. The prudish societal trends spread beyond England through Europe and as far as Gilded Age America where the upper class of the 1890s mimicked English high society. Victorian prudery needed to spread because syphilis continued to spread too, even to the Uberman himself, Friedrich Nietzsche who succumbed to the disease in 1900.

> **THINK: Do you know how to avoid contracting an STD?**

Freud's Ego

Despite the prudish society, Sigmund Freud made a name for himself in 1896 with his process of psychoanalysis. He would put patients under hypnosis and have them discuss repressed thoughts and feelings. Based on those sessions, by 1905 Freud developed his theory of sexuality stating we are all sexual beings from our infant years on. The fact that he began to look at sexuality in such a way was more significant than his conclusions, which did not all stand the test of time very well.

Freud's most lasting legacy was to divide the human psyche into three components. Your psyche is your true persona, your mind or soul or however you define yourself. The *id* is the impulsive part operating solely on the pleasure principle seeking immediate gratification. The *super ego* is the moral component looking at the right and good action to take but not factoring the context of appropriateness. The *ego* is the rational balancer of the two extremes enabling us to decide between the devil on one shoulder and the angel on the other. The id tells you to kiss your sweetheart but your super ego says no. The ego decides if you do or not.

Freud was operating during a fruitful period after the Age of Enlightenment fostered an environment for groundbreaking thought and science. Skepticism towards conventional wisdom provided an audience for his unconventional thinking. The women's suffrage movement simultaneously sought to break down traditional barriers at the turn of the 20th century. With the outbreak of World War I, women were called upon to keep the US industrial economy humming along, as most of the men went overseas to fight. That especially gave them new status in society, including the right to vote in 1919. The age of keeping women barefoot and pregnant was over.

The Roaring Twenties and a new sexual revolution were emerging. Young women who dressed differently, wore lots of makeup, and listened to jazz, comprised a popular trend known as *flappers*. Most high school students are assigned to read F. Scott Fitzgerald's *The Great Gatsby* and probably do not appreciate the scandalous portrayal of American sexuality during the period. Premarital, extramarital and other forms of sex were not written about in polite society since the beginning of the Victorian era almost a hundred years earlier. The meaningful message of this early sexual revolution is conveyed at the end of the story when the characters' lives fall into despair. The flapper life of free sex and partying was not liberating after all.

The Cultural Revolution

That message was lost on the Sixties Generation and their historic Cultural Revolution. More women entering the workforce after World War II led to more egalitarian views of the differences between the genders. Penicillin had taken care of the syphilis threat at the end of the Roaring Twenties and the introduction of the birth control pill in 1960 and legalized abortion soon afterwards enabled sexual explorations like never before. The generation that saw the Vietnam War as so misguided, came to "question authority" which included all social norms. Young people dropped out of normal society and joined groups whose purpose was to break down social conventions. The authorities who said sex was for procreation came under particular assault as American "hippy" youth engaged in "free love" meaning public nudity, group sex, bisexuality, homosexuality and anything that felt good. The Summer of Love in 1967 saw thousands gather in San Francisco. Unfortunately, the city could not support all the wayward youth who turned it into a summer of crime and violence reminiscent of the Roman Bacchanalia. Even the quintessential hippy band, The Grateful Dead, moved out of the city across the Golden Gate Bridge to Marin County.

The barn doors had been opened and there was no way to get the horses back in. Betty Freidan ignited the modern feminist movement in the early 1960s saying the portrayal of the traditional family was sexist and prevented women from fully realizing their talents in society. Birth control and abortion enabled women to pursue a career at the same time they pursued their sexuality. Some feminists celebrated their sexual liberation while others said the sexual revolution was hurting women who were becoming more objectified in the modern culture. Mothers warned their daughters that premarital sex could make them less likely to find a husband. "Why would a man buy the cow if he can get the milk for free?"

In 1969, New York City police raided a bar in Greenwich Village called The Stonewall Inn. The cause was for serving liquor without a license but the patrons and neighbors saw it as persecution of the bar's gay clientele. An ensuing series of spontaneous Stonewall Riots marked the beginning of the gay liberation movement. For the first time since ancient times, homosexuality was slowly becoming socially acceptable. Prior to Stonewall, gay people went to great efforts to hide their sexuality, as they often still do today.

Relaxed sexual norms led to successive scholarly books on the subject of human sexuality that gained mainstream readership. Sociologists William Masters and Virginia Johnson conducted a groundbreaking study of sexual practices among Americans in 1966, and six years later Alex Comfort's *The Joy of Sex* was published as a modern *Kama Sutra*. People wanted to try these new sexual practices they were reading about and the swinger subculture of sex parties provided a forum. The 21st century club culture can be traced back to the disco culture of the 1970s, although tamed considerably by the outbreak of AIDS in the 1980s. Fear of dying from AIDS put a damper on the sexual revolution like syphilis did a century earlier.

Technology also began to play its role in the development of human sexuality, if you can call it a development. Better and more prevalent movie cameras were used to produce short "stag films" of people having sex which would progress into the pornographic movie industry. The first pornographic film that gained mainstream attention was *Deep Throat* starring Linda Lovelace. She claimed to be able to do things with her throat and vagina that "other women just can't do."[17] It became hip in 1972 to go see the movie that celebrities like Jack Nicholson and even Jacqueline Kennedy Onassis went to see. Film critic Roger Ebert reviewed it saying along with his zero star rating, "If you have to work this hard at sexual freedom, maybe it isn't worth the effort." The free love lifestyle was portrayed as liberating and pleasurable but Linda Lovelace came to tell a very different story.

It is another example of sex leading to violence as she told of being forced into her career at the point of a gun. Her colleagues claim to have never seen a gun on the movie sets but did say the star often came into work baring bruises allegedly from her husband/producer.[18] In her divorce, she claimed to have been forced into prostitution by him. Regardless of the particulars, her life of sex and drugs was not a happy one. Her new trick became old and many women realized they can do the things she can do and nobody wanted to see a wrinkled old woman having sex. Linda Lovelace was addicted to drugs and had no other skills. She went on to play an active role in the anti-pornography movement but again came to feel used by its leaders.[19] Her sad and lonely life ended in a 2002 car accident.

Theology of the Body

With that history, why would anyone want to have sex? No wonder the smartest minds throughout history have seen it as getting in the way of that which is truly good. But most of them enjoyed sex. Nietzsche didn't get syphilis from riding a bicycle. This was a problem for Enlightenment philosophers and those that followed who focused on the person as an individual. It was all fine and good to extol the virtues of recognizing others as individuals but our sexual desires reduce other individuals to objects of those desires. Emanuel Kant, the 18th century German philosopher, built on Descartes' view that thinking makes us human as he applied certain principles to human sexuality to try and solve this philosophical problem about the objectification of sex. Kant said people lose their autonomy, or their individuality, in sexual acts because they are being used to give pleasure to another. He concluded that marriage resolves that problem by giving each spouse "lifelong mutual possession of their sexual characteristics."[20] However, he continued that one must not enjoy another person solely for pleasure. Kant defined sex as a union of giving oneself to another. That still objectifies the sexual partner and even goes so far as categorizing them as a possession, but he believed the mutuality makes it fair. You are learning college level material hear so don't feel intimidated if you don't get it all.

200 years later, a Polish priest living under Soviet communism would take young couples on ski and kayak trips in a ministry that taught him much about relationships and human nature. Karol Wojtyla shared his thinking in his 1960 book *Love and Responsibility* where he describes human sexuality as a gift from God. This is the polar opposite of the traditional thought that sex is the root of evil. When he became Pope John Paul II he expanded on his philosophy of human sexuality in a series of addresses that collectively became known as his *Theology of the Body*. Going back to Adam in the Garden of Eden, John Paul recognized human free will as only possible through the actions we make with our bodies. He saw our free will as a gift from God which therefore makes our bodies divine instruments that carry out our decisions.

When two people freely give themselves to each other in search for a common good, the meeting of their two freedoms is the "substance of love."[21] Unlike Kant, John Paul saw loving as using our partner to achieve a higher purpose together, a purpose built into God's design. Like Adam realized before he had Eve, our sexuality reveals a profound dependence on each other. We overcome our loneliness when we find that human counterpart that completes us. That person, our soulmate, does not inhibit our identity, they enhance it. That thought is philosophically groundbreaking enough but his theology goes further.

The complementariness of husband and wife, combined with the metaphysical euphoric experience of sexuality, revealed more to John Paul. He reminded his audiences that Jesus' most common metaphor for Heaven is a wedding feast. The Catholic Church has traditionally taught this to be a metaphor for Christ as bridegroom and the Church, or the people, as his bride; but John Paul saw more to it. This is such a common metaphor that Jesus uses, and since God made the sexual act so special to humanity, there must be more than had been contemplated by other philosophers. John Paul concluded that at the moment when we truly become one with our soulmate, the metaphysical euphoria experienced at the moment of mutual climax is a view of God; a view that philosophers have been contemplating since the dawn of humanity. This gives deeper meaning to Scripture saying that God made us in his own image, as that climax is the moment when life is made. It is the first time in the history of philosophy that sex has been seen not as a hindrance to achieving that which is good but the means to the revelation of that which is good.

THINK: Does "the substance of love" mean anything to you?

So sex is good after all, but only when it is freely and truly given as a gift of oneself within marriage. It can only be that complete gift with the commitment of marriage. Jesus never described Heaven as a hookup party. John Paul saw married couples as the "ministers of the design" that God built into procreation.[22] Since sex outside of marriage is not meant to procreate, it cannot be part of that design. Anything outside of that grand plan is contrary to natural law which is why sex so often results in dissatisfaction and shame. John Paul's theology rejects artificial birth control because it interferes with this total sharing of one another to where the conjugal act ceases to be an act of love and is rather a mere bodily union. For the same reasons, he sees premarital sex, homosexuality, masturbation, and other forms of fornication as succumbing to our base animal instincts just as so many philosophers before him did.

John Paul calls for self-mastery through chastity and temperance, and he highlights how those virtues can strengthen a marriage as couples defer to the monthly menstrual cycle to determine the best time for sexual activity. The deferment of sexual gratification also strengthens pre-marital relationships by building our willpower and leading us to find other ways to express our love for one another.

John Paul has often been criticized for demeaning sexuality but understanding his theology reveals exactly the opposite. In fact, he raises it to the level of the divine. Other critics say his views are unrealistic but he didn't present his theology as an explanation for how sex is commonly practiced, rather as an ideal to be pursued. Philosophers since the Enlightenment have explored the reason for our existence as individuals and John Paul's views on human sexuality provide much of the answer that had eluded them for more than 350 years. By stressing that we are made in God's image, he reintroduces the centrality of God into humanistic thought and Enlightenment reasoning. Our individuality and intellect do not represent a break from God as so many Enlightenment thinkers said, they are part of His grand design. That is why John Paul is recognized as a preeminent humanist philosopher which is only part of the reason he is considered the Catholic Church's fourth Great Pope and first in a thousand years.

"If you want to be loved, be lovable"

That's a 2,000 year old quote from the Roman poet Ovid and there is a lot packed into that little phrase. What does it mean to be loved? We are all loved by our parents and siblings regardless of how lovable we are. Being of the same flesh and blood naturally makes us loveable to them, even if you might not always think so. This is a chapter on sex so let's look at it that way. To enter that realm, we need to be lovable to a partner on a sexual level. In our high school years, when our bodies are experiencing raging hormones, that is sometimes easier than it should be which is why sexual activity often leads to so much dissatisfaction and confusion. Even if you are wise enough to practice the virtue of chastity and defer sexual activity, becoming lovable on a romantic level is an important part of growing up.

The Art of Love was written in the first century when the emperor Augustus was trying to instill morals in the decadent Roman society. Writing about men and women attracting each other into sexual relationships got Ovid banished to live in exile and his books were banned for millennia in polite societies worldwide, even throughout the United States until the 1960s. Ovid put each partner on equal footing in the sexual relationship which put him about 2,000 years ahead of his time. In the three books of poetic verse, he advises young men and women about how to attract and keep a lover; or in other words, how to be loveable. Reading from www.sacred-texts.com, we find the following passages that are appropriate for modern teenagers.

The first two books are addressed to men who he advises to be simple in their dress and neat in appearance. Hair and nails should be nicely trimmed and "take care that your breath is sweet." Men should not go around "reeking like a billy goat." So make sure your breath and body do not repel others. He calls for temperance when it comes to hygiene, keep yourself clean but he advises against excessive "toilet refinements" which should be left to women. In other words, men don't wear makeup.

Ovid echoes the "inscription famous throughout the world, 'Man, know thyself'" The man who knows himself will be guided by wisdom using his unique capabilities to attract the woman of his affection. Show her what you are good at, make her see your talents. An attractive man is well rounded and knowledgeable so men should enrich themselves with history and literature, like reading this book. "Ulysses was not handsome, but he was eloquent, and two goddesses were tortured with love for him."

Perhaps Ovid's most famous quote is, "Fortune and Venus favor the brave!" Venus is the goddess of love and if you want to gain her grace, then be brave. Nothing ventured nothing gained. Once you men get yourselves in order, it is time to find your lady. Only your own eye can discover the girl that suits you, a potential soulmate for you will not be one for others. When your eye catches someone, think of a way to start a conversation. "If you have a voice, sing; and if your limbs are supple, dance; in short, do everything you can to make a good impression." However, no matter how good of an impression you think you are making, don't wait for her to come to you, "'Tis for him to begin, for him to entreat her." It is one of those classic truisms throughout humanity, don't expect a pretty girl to come and pluck you from the wall you are flowering. When she catches your eye, go strike up a conversation with her.

Much of Books One and Two are about being a gentleman. Being lovable is more than just good looks, "what works wonders with women is an ingratiating manner. Brusqueness and harsh words only promote dislike." He advises to approach her by reaching for something near her and making gentle contact, "let thy hand softly encounter hers." Flatter her, say anything to win her over. Tell her how well she sings and dances and ask for more when she stops. Have only soothing words so that she may always want to be around you. "Don't give her cause to say that you're a brute." Ovid's manly man was not against showing tenderness and compassion. He said tears can "melt a diamond."

You must know what your love interest is really like, "look at her by daylight, and when you're sober." This is another way of saying do not get too caught up in the moment, someone who you are infatuated with at a party may not be as attractive when you get to know her. See how she looks and acts in different circumstances. He takes a great risk of alienating himself from women forever when he writes that "women are things of many moods." That is especially true in high school so make sure you are compatible with her personality.

Don't wait for perfect though; accept the things you do not like and become accustomed to them, "habit makes a lot of things acceptable." Real relationships take time to develop. You will find that annoyances fade while you get to know someone as their true qualities outweigh some minor quirks. Ovid advises to make yourself a habit to her by being around. "To win her heart, let no trouble be too great. Let her see you continually." When she is sick, care for her; let her know her pain hurts you too. Maybe even use some of those tears that could melt a diamond. He is saying to let her know she has reached Aristotle's highest level of friendship. Ovid was even ahead of his time when it comes to texting. He warns, "When you write, be sure and read over what you have written; many women read into a letter much more than it is intended to convey."

It's not just about what to do but also what not to do. Don't be too much of a smooth operator or "you'll frighten her and put her on her guard." Don't be too pushy either, let the right time come. If the time for sex does come, be careful. Not having the wide assortment of modern birth control available, in those days the rhythm method was mostly used. That made timing more important but timing is important for other reasons too. She may not be ready to take that step. Don't pressure your lover to do something that is not mutual. Ovid said he would not have any woman do a "duty" to him. For him, it was always about love.

Having "armed the Greeks against the Amazons" he uses Book Three to turn the favor to his female audience. It is not a reference to shopping, the Amazons were a tribe of women warriors in Greek mythology. He advises women that "a careful toilet will make you attractive, but without such attention, the loveliest faces lose their charm." He is saying that even the prettiest women must take care to keep themselves that way. Always pay attention to your personal hygiene and use makeup to "give yourself the rosy hue which Nature has denied you." He says makeup should be subtle so men do not notice. Women need to pay more attention to grooming and appearance but should keep it out of the view of men. "The art that adorns you should be unsuspected" and "there are a whole host of things we men should know nothing about."

He says that men like neatness, at least in our women. "Let your hair be nicely done. Every woman should study to find out the style that suits her best." Ovid did not care for expensive clothes as there are so many others that cost less money. "Why carry all your fortune on your back?" Remember that advice when you feel pressure from your friends to dump all your recent earnings on clothes. When you do buy clothes, also remember that "all colors are not becoming to all people." Find those colors that best complement your complexion, hair color and eyes. When you find that correct balance of hair, makeup and clothes, it is time to go out and socialize. "What avails a beautiful face if none be there to see it?"

Ovid recommended the ladies of his day go to the theater and other places of entertainment where they can meet men. To attract them he said to "let there be something feminine and gentle in your laughter, something agreeable to the ear." In addition to all the grooming and appearance advice, Ovid says men's eyes will be attracted to a woman's mannerisms, or repelled by them. "Learn how to walk as a woman should. There is a style in walking that should be carefully cultivated." As an example he references graceful dancers at the theater whose "airy lightness, charms us all." Women should also be savvy, participate in games and play them well. "I should like my pupil to know how to throw the dice with skill, and to calculate with nicety the impetus she gives them as she tosses them on to the table." There is another reason why men like women who can play games with them. "It is a bad thing for a woman not to know how to play, for love often comes into being during play." That means we get to know one another when we interact. As we get to know someone, we will realize if they could indeed be our soulmate. Interacting with others also helps us learn about ourselves. So you young ladies should not be wallflowers either.

Still, it is only half the battle merely to play well; the important thing is to be master of yourself." Ovid warns not to get too caught up in your emotions. Don't quickly fall head over heels in love for a man, he may turn out to be a rogue like Ovid. You may also reveal those aspects of your personality that you exclude from your persona. "Sometimes, when we are not properly on our guard, when we are carried away by the heat of the game, we forget ourselves and let our inmost nature stand revealed." Don't be too reserved though, playing hard to get is acceptable only to a limited extent. Ovid warns that "a haughty, disdainful look puts a man out of tune at once, and sometimes, even though a woman doesn't say a word, her countenance betrays something hostile and disagreeable." As he advises men to flatter, he advises women to flirt. "Act then, my dears, in such a way as to make us think you love us; there's nothing easier, for a man readily believes what he wants to believe."

If you do all that, your problem will be choosing which man is right for you. "Avoid the man that makes a parade of his clothes and his good looks, and is on the tenterhooks lest his hair should get ruffled." He reminds his readers that "Adonis, a simple woodlander, was the idol of a goddess." In addition to all his other advice, to attract that right guy he says to keep your body in good shape. "When you are at table, learn to be moderate and to eat a little less than you feel inclined to." That is good advice for you young men too. Try to eat a little less than you want and you will end up accumulating less fat than you want.

Ovid implores the ladies to use that same temperance when the men come calling. Don't let anyone pressure or rush you into anything. "Venus likes delay; and waiting lends an added value to your charms." Making him wait also gives you time to make sure he's right for you. Ovid advises to be choosy and do not choose too many as "too frequent harvests make the soil wax old." This has always been a truism of human nature. Men are not attracted to women who fool around a lot. They may be attracted in the way they are to a carnival ride, but not a relationship.

If you do find yourself having fully explored the sexual relationship, Ovid has a stern warning on abortion. He writes "Many a time she slays herself who slays her offspring in the womb." Like any big decision in life, ask others who have faced the same situation. You will find many women who in hindsight wished they carried their babies and put them up for adoption. As more married couples have trouble conceiving children, having babies available for adoption is more important these days than ever. Think about the joy you could bring to someone struggling with different sorrows. The joy you could give to others, and that life's potential to the world, will be many times greater than your pain. There could be no higher form of charity.

Care for Your Instrument

You will hopefully never have to contemplate such a decision and it is best advised for so many reasons to defer sexual activity in your adolescent years. Even while practicing the virtue of chastity, dating and relationships are a fundamental part of becoming an adult. Your body has reached a mature state and you naturally want to flaunt such a beautiful instrument. If it is not as beautiful as you would like, that is within your power to change. The way we keep our bodies tells others about ourselves. Most of us are not born to look like what we see in art and culture and we will never look like models. However, we can all get into a physical shape that makes us feel good which in turn makes us more attractive than if we did nothing. To do that we need to be physically active and watch what we eat.

Let's look at what that means. A 15 year old male of average height and weight will burn approximately 1,400 calories a day if he does nothing but sit around. For an average 15 year old female it is about 1,300 calories. As we get older we burn fewer calories but as we get bigger we burn more. Both of those trends work against each other as we age but the result for most of us is that we accumulate more calories than we burn. The average teenager running a quick pace for one hour will burn about 1,000 additional calories.

Calories are our bodies' energy source and we store them in our fat cells. The more calories we accumulate, the fatter we become. Some of us obviously accumulate them quicker while some burn them quicker, we are all different. Regardless of our body type, if we want to lose weight, we need to burn more calories than we consume. If it is weight gain you seek, be patient, your body will experience substantial growth in the coming years. Take care that the calories you consume and the activities you pursue will translate into the kind of body mass you want and not harmful fat cells. Working with weights or other heavy activities will support that kind of development.

We can increase the number of calories we burn daily by about half if we lead a moderately active lifestyle, meaning moderate physical activity a few days each week. We can almost double it if we have some strenuous activity every day. Joining an athletic team is a great way to accomplish that. There are so many benefits from an active lifestyle beyond the calorie burn rate. Physical activity brings us places where we meet other people and learn about the world. It causes our brains and bodies to produce hormones and chemicals that make us feel better, the famous "runner's high." We gain confidence from working hard to improve ourselves. Our bodies, even if overweight or underdeveloped, look better when we exercise and we gain energy from carrying around a fitter load. Then we don't want to eat as much and it becomes a virtuous cycle.

Making a habit of daily exercise will keep you physically fit and also help you think better. Physical activity is a great way to unwind your frustrations and keep a peaceful mind. Even if you are not athletic, joining a team will bring you these great benefits while teaching you how to achieve goals and work with teammates. Our bodies are our greatest asset so it only makes sense to take care of them.

> **THINK: What is your favorite way to exercise?**

Reducing our caloric intake is as important as increasing our burn rate. We consume most of our calories at breakfast, lunch and dinner which is usually more than we need before considering snacks and treats. Be aware of the food you eat because it is true what they say, you are what you eat. One way to do that is to help prepare dinner at home and learn how to cook. You will gain a better understanding of what you are feeding yourself and build an important skill for later in life. Being aware of the spontaneous food we eat is very important too. Those calories add up quickly and they are harder to take off than put on.

Quenching every thirst with a sugary drink will create a habit that adds pounds over time. When you must have that sweet drink, drink some water first so the sugary treat lasts longer and leaves you more satisfied. Drinking plenty of water with your meals will also make you feel satisfied while eating less. Remember Ovid's advice to eat a little less than we want. Even if you continue to indulge in that afternoon snack, being aware of its effect on your body will help you better know yourself. Of course all calories are not equal, the 150 that come from an apple and orange are better than the same number that come from a bag of chips. But you don't need a book to tell you that.

Taking care of your body will make you attractive to others and you will more easily catch someone's eye. To get to their heart, you need to be more than just physically lovable. Nobody is going to love you if you do not love yourself and show love to others. We should love the gift of life like the greatest gift we have ever received, because it is. Developing our talents and our better attributes makes our lives richer and makes it easier to love ourselves. Recognizing our own qualities helps us to recognize lovable qualities in others. Living the seven virtues is how you love yourself and others. Living virtuously gives you the confidence to handle life's adversity. You will have greater empathy for the emotional needs of those you love. Loving others is how you become more lovable yourself.

Your Brain on Love

Tom Petty sang that even the losers get lucky sometime so keep making yourself more lovable and someone will find your good habits attractive enough to pursue you as their love interest. Love is the lucky part and you may not want to hear it, but sex often gets in the way. That's why Plato preferred the beauties of the soul to those of the body. People who share love but not sex are said to have a Platonic relationship and modern science has discovered reasons why it is ideal for teenagers.

The increased thrill seeking among teens discussed in the last chapter arises from the way our brains secrete a neurotransmitter called dopamine, which is a chemical that enables your brain cells to communicate with one another. A teenage brain has a wider range of dopamine secretions, lower lows and higher highs, than children and adults which causes teenagers to experience wider emotional swings.[23] When the dopamine levels are low, we get bored; excitement makes them spike. This explains why teens are often bored unless engaging in stimulating activity.

Not many activities are more stimulating than sex, so teenagers have a propensity to engage in sexual activity in circumstances when adults would not. Such as with a partner who is not worthy of such sharing. It is not just our brains, but our bodies are also experiencing changes that turbocharge our sexual arousal. Increased hormonal levels disrupt an otherwise balanced body chemistry making us feel attracted to others more easily and needing sexual release. Males experience that literally with wet dreams and unwelcome erections. It is why most teens feel the temptation to masturbate.

Remember, teens weigh reward much higher than risk and often those rewards come from admiration among our peers. The common caricature of peer pressure portrays teens admonishing their friends to do something they don't want to do. As you probably know already, it is usually more subtle than that, and even subconscious. We think our friends will admire us when we have sex, so we weigh that more highly than the risk that we may hurt ourselves by contracting an STD or hurt our partner who may not be ready to take such a step. Children and adults have mechanisms in their brains that calm emotional swings but teens lack that regulating process and sexual activity is prone to supercharge our emotions.[24]

That is especially true with sexual intercourse when our feelings are intensified from the secretion of the hormone oxytocin. For females it may manifest as an intensification of bonding or connectedness but it can also lead to intense jealousy and aggression. This is one reason why sexual activity so often causes such distress in the lives of teens. The lower areas of a teenage brain are more active than adults and that's the part of the brain that leads to these rapidly arising and intense emotions. This is why it is so easy for teens to misinterpret one another. You may think your love interest is for the long term while he or she may see the relationship as a short term exploration. It is best to be sure both are on the same page before you regret any actions you take. We will see later that children and adults have a more active prefrontal cortex, the brain's source of calming effects. Therefore teens need to think things through more carefully.

Love is wonderful when it happens but don't get too despondent when it doesn't. You may meet your soulmate in high school but you are much more likely to experience the loss of love and that is not all bad. Your life ahead will hopefully be a joyous one but all lives have times of pain and stress. Experiencing that at a younger age will make your foundation stronger, like it did for Lincoln. You still want to avoid unpleasant circumstances. That is why Platonic relationships are so good for adolescents. As your teenage brain becomes more able to process complex situations, exploring yourself and the meaning of life with a true friend will prepare you for a more fulfilling romantic relationship later. You learn about the attributes necessary to maintain a relationship that go deeper than pleasures of the body. Having a relationship provides an avenue for selflessness as you attempt to reach that highest form of friendship. You will also learn about those qualities you value most highly so when you eventually do find your soulmate, you will be wise enough to recognize them as such.

Many teens have questions about their own sexuality that are best answered before proceeding down a path that could be painful. Homosexual tendencies may indicate an innate nature or could just be a teenage brain exploring a variety of emotions. You may tend toward a domineering mate or a relationship where you are the dominant partner, or the most common arrangement where each partner dominates different aspects of the relationship. Experience and time will reveal your true innateness and that self-knowledge will be clearer without the fog of sex. When your search eventually leads to certainty, you will be more likely to find a fulfilling relationship if you have been patient and diligent in your thinking.

As you find yourself exploring the wonderful and astonishing world of sex, do so in accordance with knowing yourself. If that means achieving the sexual release only with yourself, that is better than hurting someone else that you care about in a selfish act of personal gratification. Take care not to hurt yourself either, make sure a sexual partner is prepared to totally share themselves like you are. Hooking up may seem easy and pleasurable but know that such sex is just that and not love. It is merely glorified masturbation with a lot more risk to yourself and your partner. Don't worry about what your friends are doing and saying. Much of it is lies and the others are likely exaggerating the experience. If you do find yourself fully exploring a sexual relationship, be careful. Make sure it is done in an environment of sharing and trust, if not love. Know your natural teenage susceptibility to wild emotions and recognize them when they occur. Follow your conscience and as always, do what is right.

Chapter 4: Drugs

For sensible men I prepare only three kraters:
one for health (which they drink first), the second
for love and pleasure, and the third for sleep.
After the third one is drained, wise men go home.
The fourth krater is not mine any more - it
belongs to bad behavior; the fifth is for shouting;
the sixth is for rudeness and insults; the seventh is
for fights; the eighth is for breaking the furniture;
the ninth is for depression; the tenth is for
madness and unconsciousness.

- Dionysus, Greek god of wine

Not much remains of the work by the ancient Greek comic Eubulus, but his words above certainly apply to the modern world. Dionysus was the Greek counterpart to Bacchus, the Roman god of wine. Written around the time Socrates was teaching virtue to the youth of Athens, the passage exemplifies the virtue of temperance and the dangers of gluttony. Wise men limited their consumption and hardship followed those that didn't. We have seen how that applies to love and sex which are the subjects of Plato's *Symposium* whose title is the Greek word for a drinking party. Plato uses a victory celebration in a poetry festival to set the scene for a discussion on the nature of love. Drinking helps the characters open up and express their true feelings but we also see jealousy arise when some open up too much. As the wisest among them, Socrates can keep drinking after all the others have fallen asleep, yet he does not get drunk or hung over the next day. Of course, the story is allegorical as drinking to excess will give anyone a hangover, or sick feeling the next day. Like Plato's characters, you will likely regret some things you say or do while having your consciousness impaired.

Drinking parties were an integral part of ancient Greek society and have been important to most societies since. A typical ancient Greek symposium would see a group of up to twenty men from the higher echelons of society assemble after dinner in comfortable surroundings and share an initial cup of wine in homage to the gods, before engaging in intellectual conversation. The wine back then was stronger than today's and was usually diluted with water in a type of pitcher referenced as a krater above. The host would increase the proportion of water as the night wore on. Those in other social classes undoubtedly had other ways of getting inebriated and although there were no distilled spirits, or liquor, back then, we know they had access to some of the same drugs that exist today. Whether looking at the elite of ancient Greece or common workers in any other society, the history of drug use is a long one, so don't forget to take a break at a section header as we explore how humans have altered their minds through time.

Joy Plants

In Homer's *Odyssey* we see a reference to "nepenthe" explained as a drug of forgetfulness which probably referred to a mixture of wine and opium. Homer says *"those who drank of the mixture did not shed a tear all day long, even if their mother or father had died, even if a brother or beloved son was killed before their eyes by the weapons of the enemy."*[25] That would certainly describe opium which will numb any pain. It had been used for thousands of years before the ancient Greeks and derives from the poppy flower. The earliest known reference to opium is from a Sumerian tablet dating from around 4000 BC in Mesopotamia, so it is at least as old as writing itself. It was called a "joy plant" to be used not only medicinally but also recreationally and ritualistically.

Hippocrates, the Father of Medicine, lived in ancient Greece and began the practice of identifying disease as a product of environmental factors rather than punishment from the gods. Medical students to this day take a Hippocratic Oath upon earning their degree. The oath has changed over the centuries but is often summarized as "First, do no harm." Hippocrates did not recognize the harm from opium and used the drug as a cure for many ailments. The word narcotic derives from the Greek word *narkotikos* which means "to numb." He and the medical professionals that followed have used opium to numb people suffering from chronic pain. Unfortunately many of those people then become addicted to the painkiller. Prescription painkillers are the source of so much of today's opioid epidemic as the powerful drug exerts its influence beyond medicine.

Plants are the source of other drugs you have heard about too. Archeologists have found South American pottery from 3000 BC showing people chewing coca leaves in religious rituals and burials. People living in the Andes Mountains chewed the leaves for endurance at the high altitudes where they lived, and began to cultivate it around 1000 AD. It became incorporated into the spiritual and political structure of the early Incan Empire 500 years later when Europe was enjoying the Renaissance. Spanish conquistadors who invaded Peru brought coca back to Europe but it was not processed into cocaine until 1844. It too was initially seen as a wonder drug. One of the most famous doctors of the late 1800s, Sigmund Freud, was a vocal advocate of cocaine since it helped him cure his depression. He called it "the magical substance" and prescribed it for many of his patients including relatives and friends.

Marijuana also dates back thousands of years with the earliest known reference in a pharmacy book by Chinese emperor Shen Nung from 2737 BC. It came to the new world around 1545 when Spanish conquistadors brought it to Chile. It was also introduced as hemp into Virginia's Jamestown colony in 1611 to be cultivated for its fiber, oil and seeds to make a variety of everyday necessities like rope, cloth, lamp oil and birdseed. The early

American agricultural economy was so reliant on hemp that Virginians were compelled to grow it. George Washington complied and his journal suggests he found use for it beyond making rope. He referenced separating the male from female plants which was generally done to increase the potency of its mind altering properties.

The American colonists had other opportunities to alter their consciousness as an assortment of liquors became available. The early settlers drank beer and hard cider but simple fermentation could not produce a drink much stronger than wine. Distilled spirits had first been developed around 800 AD but didn't become common in the new world until inland farmers found the cost of transporting their grain to the coastal markets was almost as much as the price they fetched. Fermenting and distilling the grain into whiskey was a lucrative way to add value to their crop. Rev. Elijah Craig aged whiskey in charred oak barrels and began the industry named for the county where he lived in the late 1700s, Bourbon Kentucky. Sugar cane farmers in the Caribbean also found that distilling their product into rum provided a similarly valuable end product for their agriculture. New Englanders liked it so much that their colonies became big importers of molasses to distill into rum which developed into a major export of the early American economy.

The biggest export from 17th century America was tobacco. Colonist John Rolfe is most famous for his marriage to the daughter of a powerful Indian chief who had been captured by the settlers and held for ransom. When the chief didn't pay, Pocahontas converted to Christianity and married the wealthy tobacco farmer. It may be the first interracial marriage in America and became a symbol of the peace that could exist between the settlers and Native Americans. Pocahontas might not have been too distraught about moving into a fine home with all the comforts of wealth. She became internationally famous before dying at a young age while traveling in Europe.

Christopher Columbus had brought tobacco back to Europe as a gift from the Native Americans he encountered on his first trip to the new world. The uniquely American crop became a hit throughout Europe and the nicotine in tobacco remains one of the world's most used drugs today. It is so widely used that most people do not even consider it a drug although it is by most definitions. So is another product loved and consumed in large quantities by most Americans, coffee.

According to legend, coffee was discovered in 900 AD when an Arabian shepherd noticed his goats bouncing around after eating certain red berries. The shepherd tried some and word of its effects spread through Africa and beyond over the following centuries. The caffeine in coffee had already been a popular stimulant in the form of tea for the American colonists who were as hooked on it as other societies were. That made tea a good product for Britain's King George III to asses with a tax. This was obviously not popular among the colonists who were getting tired of the king's taxation without representation, meaning they had no say in the taxes levied against them. A group of revolutionaries calling themselves the Sons of Liberty, disguised as Indians, boarded a merchant vessel in Boston Harbor, and threw all of its cargo of British tea overboard. Ever since the Boston Tea Party in 1773, America has been a land of coffee drinkers, although not just coffee as the most famous Son of Liberty, Samuel Adams, has been immortalized by the popular beer named for him.

More Addictive Than Tea

The British people remained avid consumers of tea in addition to other products from the Far East. The British East India Company was the world's first international corporation and did very well importing tea, spices, silk and other exotic goods. So well that King George was getting worried about all the British silver that was ending up in Asia in exchange for all those products. He put pressure on the merchants to find a way to reverse the currency imbalance. They found a good business in trading opium from India for silver and gold to replace that which they traded for tea, silk and all the other products the British people wanted. China's mostly closed economy forced the merchants to use Chinese people to transport the opium across the country to the popular ports for British vessels. That had the added benefit of getting millions of Chinese hooked on the drug. By the middle of the 19th century, all those addicts provided enough silver to fund Victorian England.

Now the Chinese emperor was the one worrying about China's depleting silver stocks just as he needed to fight rebellions at home. A nation of opium addicts only added to his worries. He appointed an official to end the Chinese trade in opium who made a case beyond the economic issues relating to trade imbalances. Lin Zexu wrote an open letter to Queen Victoria, the British monarch by that time, largely based on Confucian concepts of morality and spirituality. He highlighted the barbarian profiteers who have no concern for the plight they leave behind and Victoria's own prohibition on the drug in England. He finished his letter asking "where is your conscience?" It is doubtful that the queen received the letter before Lin's agents seized the cargo of a British ship anchored off the banks of the Pearl River outside Humen Town, in 1839. As the world's only naval power, Britain could not tolerate having its ships' sovereignty violated and the first Opium war was afoot. It lasted about three and a half years. Similar issues relating to pride and greed set off the Second Opium War which began in 1856 and ended in 1860.

Dope Fiend's Paradise

By that point, Americans were well adept at getting intoxicated. All the latest liquors the world had to offer were creating a lot of alcoholics in the young nation. Opium was the popular treatment for alcoholism as it was commonly claimed that "alcohol maddens, opium soothes." Of course that created a lot of opium addicts who were seen as preferable to alcoholics. In 1805 a German pharmacist isolated the active ingredient in opium creating a new "wonder drug" seen as a non-addicting cure for opium addiction. He named the drug after the Greek god of dreams, Morpheus, but he was wrong about the non-addictive characteristics of morphine. About 100 years later, morphine would be processed further into heroin which was originally marketed as a non-addictive morphine substitute. Throughout history people always think they can handle their intoxicants, while they become enslaved by them.

Many writers of the early 19th century became addicted to a popular drink called laudanum which combined alcohol and morphine or other opiates. Thomas DeQuincy published his *Confessions of an English Opium-Eater* in 1821 chronicling the pleasures and the pains of his opium addiction. The section on the pains was longer than the pleasures and included the author's experiences with insomnia, nightmares and physical pain. People focused more on the pleasures section however and it became widespread knowledge that many of the great writers of the era were under the influence of what was in fact a hard drug.

Laudanum was sold widely around the country in various forms of "patent medicines." Slick talking salesmen would come to town hawking their secret formulas that cured all the worst ailments. It usually worked as opium will numb any pains of the body and mind. They didn't tell their customers about the addictive nature of the ingredients and housewives across the country were becoming opium addicts. The great actress Katherine Hepburn played such a character in Eugene O'Neil's *A Long Day's Journey Into Night*. Set in the early 20th century, the play is an exposition on addiction and the trouble it causes families. We see resentments, bitterness and attempts at affection fall back into recriminations. One of the sons tells how difficult it is to have a "dope fiend for a mother." It is considered to be the playwright's masterpiece.

When opium began to get a bad name, cocaine filled the void. Not just Sigmund Freud but all sorts of reputable members of society saw the extract from coca leaves as a healthy stimulant. A wine infused with coca was sold in the late 19th century with endorsements from Thomas Edison and Pope Leo XIII.[26] The world's most respected kings and princes similarly endorsed the product. Another beverage featuring coca extracts combined with highly caffeinated extracts of the kola nut was fast becoming the world's most popular drink. Atlanta's Coca-Cola was advertised as an "Intellectual Beverage and Temperance Drink" and "a valuable Brain Tonic and cure for all nervous afflictions."[27] It had the added benefit to its makers of addicting their customers to the product. All the freely available drugs and alcohol led one sociologist to describe 19th century America as a "dope fiend's paradise."[28] Coca-Cola dropped the coca extracts from the formula in the early 20th century.

The Rise of Temperance

Sensibilities began to change towards the end of the 19th century. Many soldiers returning home from the Civil War were addicted to the morphine they were given to sooth their battle wounds. It was so common that opium addiction became known as "soldiers' disease." Smoking opium was also common among the Chinese laborers imported to build the nation's railroads. They established opium dens where they consumed the drug and housewives addicted to patent medicines became frequent patrons. That didn't please their husbands who pushed for prohibitions that fed on the fear of foreigners importing their dangerous habits. They found success in the late 1800s when several states instituted opium prohibitions of varying degrees. We will see how other drug laws gained support by drawing on fears about foreigners.

Cocaine was also falling out of favor and even Sigmund Freud denounced his earlier advocacy of the drug. Although he claimed to have never become addicted, several of his friends did. One of them took it on his advice and developed a full-fledged cocaine psychosis complete with hallucinations of snakes crawling all over his skin.[29] Even when only a small percentage of users have such adverse effects, it still amounts to a very large number of people, so word of cocaine's dangers spread.

With the turning of sentiment, the world needed an alternative to the commonly used narcotics and Adolf von Baeyer, a German Nobel Prize winning chemist and founder of the pharmaceutical company bearing his name, discovered one when he combined malonic acid with urea in 1862. The story says he used the urine of a barmaid he loved named Barbara and called his concoction "Barbara's Urats." Barbiturates and the also newly developed amphetamines became widely used medical replacements for cocaine and other narcotic stimulants.

Irish immigrants in the middle of the 19th century brought their unique drinking habits to America and met resistance from society similar to their Chinese predecessors. Temperance movements that had existed for decades gained prominence late in the century. The most powerful of them was the Woman's Christian Temperance Union organized in 1873. Temperance organizations appealed to women for a number of reasons. Not only were women succumbing more frequently to the ravages of drug addiction but they were also bearing abuse from drunken husbands.

Those fighting against alcohol consumption raised funds to install drinking fountains in cities so men would not need to enter saloons to get refreshment. Temperance fountains, like the one still standing in New York City's Tomkins Square Park, often featured Hebe, the Greek goddess of youth atop a canopy adorned with the words "Faith, Hope, Charity and Temperance." More significant than the drinking fountains, the major achievement of the temperance movement was the Eighteenth Amendment to the United States Constitution. Ratified in 1920, Prohibition banned alcohol consumption throughout the United States.

Reefer Madness

The history is clear that Prohibition did not stop people from drinking. Quite the opposite, since it became more difficult to acquire, consumption skewed away from beer and wine towards the more potent distilled spirits. In 1986, marijuana activist

Richard Cowen coined his "Iron Law of Prohibition" stating that as law enforcement becomes more intense, the potency of the prohibited substance increases. In his words, "the harder the enforcement, the harder the drugs." He was referring to marijuana laws but Prohibition proved it applies to alcohol too.

Marijuana was legal during Prohibition so those unable to get opium or alcohol found pot to be the best substitute. It was also used medicinally and from 1850 until 1942 was listed in the United States Pharmacopeia, which sets the standards for all medications and health care products sold in the country. It was recommended for a variety of ailments and as an aphrodisiac and appetite stimulant. Although references to recreational marijuana use appear in the 19th century, it did not become popular until Prohibition when "tea pads," a name for smoking establishments, began to spring up. It is estimated that New York City had 500 such establishments in 1930; many of them were exclusive gentlemen's clubs.

Marijuana use among the newly arriving Mexican immigrant population, and the increases in crime that came with them, brought the popular new drug into the focus of the temperance movement. Since crime was increasing in areas with large Mexican immigrant populations, and marijuana was popular among them, it was surmised that smoking marijuana led to crime. As we can see from history, if Mexican laborers didn't bring marijuana to Americans in the early 20th century, someone else would have.

As anti-Mexican sentiment drove the movement opposing marijuana use, the American political landscape was turning against Prohibition and all the crime that came with it. Franklin D. Roosevelt ran for President in 1932 opposing Prohibition as well as reinvigorating the economy suffering in the early years of the Great Depression. He kept his campaign promise by supporting the Twenty-first Amendment to the Constitution which was ratified on December 5, 1933. Section 1 of the Twenty-first Amendment reads: "The eighteenth article of amendment to the Constitution of the United States is hereby repealed." The thirteen year experiment in alcohol prohibition was over. Now that alcohol was legal again and with many states enacting marijuana prohibitions, use of the latter declined.

President Roosevelt needed to remain in the good graces of the temperance movement so he did not discourage the head of the Federal Bureau of Narcotics (now the Drug Enforcement Administration) from his campaign to criminalize marijuana use. Some claim that Harry Anslinger was acting at the behest of powerful financial interests who wanted to eliminate low cost hemp that competed with their newly invented industrial products, such as nylon. The modern industrial products would have won out anyway and thankfully World War II paratroopers didn't have to use parachutes made from hemp. Whatever his motivations, Anslinger became one of the most powerful men in the country while he held his office from 1930 until 1962. The governing laws relating to narcotics in 1930 included the Pure Food and Drug Act of 1906 which established the Food and Drug Administration and largely eliminated the patent medicines being sold around the country. The Harrison Narcotics Act of 1914 banned the sale of opium and coca based substances, except in limited medical uses. Marijuana only came under the purview of various state laws.

Anslinger wanted to change that, so he led a national campaign to demonize the drug. Propaganda films like *Reefer Madness* portrayed it as a "deadly narcotic worse than opium, heroin and morphine." After smoking pot, the film's characters engage in dangerous and violent behavior that leads to death for some and insanity for others. The effective campaign led Congress to hold brief hearings in 1937 where few voices were heard in opposition to national marijuana prohibition. Sellers of birdseed that contained marijuana seeds were among the few that did testify in opposition saying: "We have never found another seed that makes a bird's coat so lustrous or makes them sing so much." Anslinger testified in favor of the legislation saying "Marijuana is an addictive drug which produces in its users insanity, criminality, and death." The Marijuana Tax Act of 1937 easily passed on an unrecorded vote despite the opposition of the American Medical

Association. In later years, Anslinger had to concede that the threat from marijuana is primarily as a gateway to other worse drugs. So smoking pot will not turn you into a criminal or make you insane and it certainly will not kill you, but it does present plenty of risks to a teenager which we will explore later.

Turn On, Tune In, Drop Out

Use of both agricultural hemp and recreational pot declined until the 1960s Cultural Revolution, seen from the sexual angle in the previous chapter. Youths questioning authority and veterans returning from the Vietnam War were enjoying not just traditional drugs but new ones that came to define the era. In 1943, a Swiss scientist named Albert Hoffman working for the Sandoz pharmaceutical company accidentally discovered lysergic acid, or LSD, and its powerful psychoactive effects. After getting some of the experimental compound on his fingers, he described an "intoxicated-like condition, characterized by an extremely stimulated imagination" and "an uninterrupted stream of fantastic pictures, extraordinary shapes with intense, kaleidoscopic play of colors."[30] Sandoz appointed him director of their natural products department where he continued studying hallucinogenic substances like psilocybin found in certain mushrooms which were used as early as 1000 BC among the Aztecs in Guatemala.

Timothy Leary, a clinical psychology professor at Harvard University, began holding off campus sessions with students where they would experiment with LSD which had yet to be made illegal. Those unable to join the sessions acquired the substance on the black market that was exploding along with the Sixties counterculture. Leary and poet Allan Ginsburg set out to introduce the drug to intellectuals and artists and became celebrities associated with the drug culture. In front of 30,000 San Francisco hippies in 1967, Leary coined the phrase "Turn on, tune in, drop out" which came to define the era's drug culture.

There were other new drugs too. As the addictive tendencies of barbiturates and amphetamines became recognized, new prescription drugs like Quaaludes and Valium were developed. The Rolling Stones recorded a hit song about Valium in 1965 called *Mothers Little Helper*. Ten years later, Valium was the world's most prescribed drug. The growing drug culture led to the 1970 Comprehensive Drug Abuse Prevention and Control Act which forms the basis of today's drug laws. Drug abuse was becoming so ingrained in American culture that President Richard Nixon declared it "public enemy number one" when he launched his War on Drugs in 1971.

A volunteer soldier in that war was Elvis Presley, who reached out to President Nixon and arranged a meeting on December 21, 1970 to express his patriotism and contempt for the hippies and their drug culture. Elvis represented the other side of the Cultural Revolution. He was among those who cherished American traditions. Born in Tupelo Mississippi in 1935, his twin brother died at birth and his father served a short prison term for an innocuous offence. Facts that may account for an exceptionally strong bond he held with his mother. The family lived in the African-American neighborhoods of the various towns they called home, which exposed Elvis to the unique rhythm and blues music of the region. Instead of the bicycle or rifle he hoped for, he got a guitar for his seventh birthday which some uncles and the family's pastor taught him to play. He was especially shy about his playing but worked up enough courage to bring his guitar to school when he was in seventh grade. It took courage because he was bullied as a trashy momma's boy who played hillbilly music, but he kept on developing his emerging talent. By twelve years old he found a mentor who taught him some chord techniques and arranged for him to perform on the radio. He became overwhelmed with stage fright but managed to perform on his second attempt a week later.

As a teenager in Memphis, Tennessee, Elvis was immersed in the blues music that made the city famous. He overcame his shyness and took a liking to the stage after getting a job as an usher in the local theater. He had other jobs too because a poor teenager couldn't ask his parents for money. Elvis worked hard and always kept busy. High school brought him into circles of friends who also enjoyed music and he chose his friends well. A couple of upper classmen taught him how to be a better guitar player and went on to illustrious careers in music themselves. Spending some of his time and earnings at Memphis blues clubs, the ambitious and diligent teenager made friendships with singers who would become legendary, like B.B. King who became the "King of the Blues" long before Elvis became the "King of Rock and Roll." Having a strong bond with his parents, respect for mentors and a clear sense of where he wanted to go, Elvis was on a good path in life. However, the virtuous work ethic didn't extend to school where he got a C in eighth grade music. He spoke about it later in his career as "failing music" so it must have stung to score so poorly in his life's calling. He played by ear without ever learning to read music, and in junior year of high school, he entered a talent show. He was amazed at how popular he became after people recognized his talents. It must have been an incredible dopamine rush because he kept working on his hobby. By the time he graduated high school, he knew that music was going to be his future.

Sam Philips' Sun Records Studio was where artists got famous and Elvis saved enough money to record some songs for his mother there. There were less expensive studios in Memphis but Elvis was hoping to be discovered by the city's hottest record producer, and he was. A radio appearance followed when Mr. Phillips asked Elvis what high school he attended, as a way to tell the audience that Elvis wasn't the latest black musician. Black performers had no chance of commercial success in the segregated south and some of them resented Elvis for becoming famous by singing their music, others appreciated him for making their music popular. He was controversial for that, but more for the way he danced and shook his hips. Nobody had ever seen anything like it. Traditionalists hated the sexual suggestiveness of his performances while Rock & Roll was criticized for its general assault on conventional norms.

The critics only fed his popularity and Elvis became the first star to bond particularly with America's youth. When asked about all the controversy he was causing, he said "I don't feel like I'm doing anything wrong. ... I don't see how any type of music would have any bad influence on people when it's only music. ... I mean, how would rock 'n' roll music make anyone rebel against their parents?"[31] He was becoming a symbol of the emerging Cultural Revolution that he never embraced. His TV appearances would be limited to waist up only so nobody could see his gyrating hips. It was his first appearance on the hugely popular Ed Sullivan Show that shot him to stardom even though the show's host had declared Elvis to be "unfit for family viewing."[32] By the time of his third appearance on the show, Elvis had reached the height of controversy with protests anywhere he appeared. It was taking an emotional toll on the young man simply trying to pursue his talent. The Sixties had yet to arrive but divisions were forming in America between traditionalists and a young generation declaring themselves agents of change. Elvis didn't want to be political, he just loved music and by now he also loved to entertain. After that third performance, Ed Sullivan walked on stage, put his arm around Elvis and told America that he was "a real decent, fine boy."[33] With that endorsement from such a bright light of American tradition, the protests quieted down.

Further acceptance came when Elvis was drafted into the U.S. Army and didn't try to get out of it like most famous people did. Before the Viet Nam War and the anti-war protest movement would energize the Cultural Revolution, Elvis was establishing his persona as the all-American boy. He went on to serve for two years, stationed in Germany where he met his future wife Priscilla. He told her how he feared his service would ruin his career but exactly the opposite happened. His absence made America's heart grow fonder for him, while his managers strategically released songs that he had recorded before leaving for Germany. When he came home from his military service, he began acting in movies and became the biggest star of stage and screen that the world had ever seen.

He seemed to be making all the right choices but ironically, the all-American superstar was becoming a drug addict himself. He began using amphetamines while in the Army. Many soldiers used the general issue medications back then and Elvis actually promoted them for increased energy and weight loss. It's understandable that he didn't see anything wrong with doing what his military commanders advocated. When he reached out to help with President Nixon's War on Drugs, he had already been hooked for a decade. By 1973 he had become terribly addicted as he struggled with a divorce from Priscilla. Twice that year he overdosed on barbiturates, in one case leading to a three day coma. Another time, he was hospitalized in a semi-comatose state from an addiction to Demerol, a narcotic pain reliever. His final years saw Elvis as a bloated mess unable to remember lyrics to his songs and cutting concerts short or missing some altogether. The all-American boy who worked hard and developed his talents, nevertheless fell victim to drug addiction. He became a symbol of the risks of drug abuse while he was still alive.

According to his doctor, Elvis did not see himself as a drug addict because the drugs were medically prescribed. They took a toll on his body nonetheless and the King of Rock & Roll was found dead on August 16, 1977 at the age of 42. Lab reports after his death found fourteen drugs in his system, with ten in significant quantity. Having caused such harm, his doctor subsequently lost his license for overprescribing drugs. He never practiced medicine again.

Drugs from the medicine cabinet have proven to be just as dangerous as those from the street. The pharmaceutical industry has been adept at responding to the concerns of their customers while continuing to give them what they want. When the patent for Valium was nearing expiration, Xanex was developed and introduced in 1981, and similar drugs have followed. As we saw earlier, much of today's heroin epidemic has resulted from people becoming addicted to prescription pain killers. It's a short distance from the medicine cabinet to the street. Be very careful if you ever sustain an injury that necessitates powerful painkillers. It is one of many ways that people can fall victim to addiction.

A new form of cocaine hit the streets in the 1980s called crack. It was smoked primarily by inner city addicts and became associated with rising crime. Teens who are not allowed in bars fueled the rave culture in the 1990s where more dangerous drugs like ecstasy became prevalent. 21st century Americans consume more drugs than ever and various new synthetic ones have hit the streets. Bath salts and synthetic marijuana like K2 and Spice have been associated with several instances of psychotic episodes that are similar to PCP or Angel Dust which wreaked havoc in American cities during the crack epidemic. As another example of the Iron Law of Prohibition, recent years have witnessed new highly potent drugs like methamphetamine and salvia which lead to more dangerous behavior and oftentimes tragic consequences for teens and young adults. The history of drug use has culminated in the heroin epidemic of recent years that has so ravaged America. If any good could come from such a sad period in American history, maybe others will recognize the risks and resist the temptation to try.

THINK: Has your life been touched by addiction?

They Call It Dope for a Reason

There must be a reason why people engage in such dangerous behavior and as we have seen in earlier chapters, it comes down to the dopamine in our brains. Advances in medical imaging over recent years have given scientists a view of the human brain never before seen. Those advancements have shown the unique ways the teenage brain processes information through the chemicals it produces. In the following section, you will gain knowledge never known to your parents, teachers and most people older than your generation. Understanding what is happening with your brain will help you navigate these challenging years in a way your predecessors did not even imagine. It is high level, modern science, so try to follow along attentively.

Dopamine is a chemical called a neurotransmitter that helps brain cells communicate with one another. This communication happens through neural circuits and the ones that use dopamine are more active in our adolescent years. We have seen that teens have lower lows and higher highs which increases impulsiveness and the drive for thrills. This is also why teens tend to focus more on the rewards of a certain activity and neglect to put that in the context of the broader risks. The wider dopamine ranges during these years also make teens more vulnerable to addiction. Drugs and alcohol cause dopamine to be released and when it wears off, the levels plummet. We then feel more of a need to use the same substance to get those levels back up.[34] There is even evidence that this can happen when we eat junk food or play video games.

Dr. Daniel J. Siegel, MD, a clinical professor of psychiatry at the UCLA School of Medicine, has published extensive research on the teenage brain in a series of bestselling books. He has a model of the brain that we all carry around with us, our hand. If you make a fist with your thumb under your fingers, it forms a shape similar to your brain. In his book *Brainstorm: The Power and Purpose of the Teenage Brain*, Dr. Siegel explains the enormously complex brain processes in a simple way with his "handy" brain model.[35] Your fingers represent your brain's cortex, the top of the brain. It provides the ability to think and reflect, perceive and plan and make decisions. Your self-awareness comes from this cortical region. Just under that area is your thumb, representing your limbic area controlling your motivations, memory and how you focus your attention. The palm is the lowest area called the brainstem involved with basic functions like keeping you awake or letting you sleep. The limbic area and brainstem are together called the sub cortical region and are responsible for base emotions like anger and fear. The wrist represents the spinal cord linking the brain with the rest of your body.[36]

Not represented in the hand model is the cerebellum behind the limbic area playing an important role in balancing the body's motions and the interactions of your thoughts and feelings. This lower part of your brain influences emotional, motivational, evaluative, and memory systems that operate in the model's thumb. It is where your brain produces dopamine from a gland in the brainstem area called the *nucleus accumbens*. Dopamine also pushes up into your cortex to influence your thinking, decision making, and behavior.

Moving to the forehead, your fingertips represent the prefrontal cortex linking all the other regions to one another. It is where you integrate all the information in your brain regarding a given situation. Most importantly, this is the part of the brain being remodeled in your adolescent years. The remodeling process impedes the functioning of the rest of the cortex that helps you think clearly and deeply about things. This natural and necessary maturing process inhibits your ability to assess a situation and reason through it and to pause and reflect on what is going on.[37] That's because the part of your brain that does all that is under construction. It doesn't mean you are unable to do those things, you just need to be more conscious and think more carefully than you otherwise would. The cortex, especially the front part, is called the executive region because executives need to manage multiple information streams and make constant decisions. The remodeling process is one reason why teenagers don't make good executives.

> **THINK: Have you ever felt like your brain isn't functioning properly?**

Under Construction

Pruning the brain's excess neurotransmitters during adolescence leads to a process of *myelination* where membranes of a substance called myelin grow over interlinked neurons in your brain to allow faster and more synchronized information flow.[38] Think of a path being paved over to make a highway. This pruning and myelination make the brain more integrated which helps you think more intuitively, like an executive does. Your brain actually grows fibers of cognitive control that help you think through a situation and act less impulsively.[39] It is part of the natural process we all go through and like the rest of your body, you want to keep it healthy and fit. Introducing drugs and alcohol during this time integrates the substances into the brain's processes which makes teens much more susceptible to addiction.[40] You don't want your brain's dopamine secretions to become dependent on an outside substance. In the next section, we will see how some teens were able to handle drugs and alcohol without realizing they had been enslaved by deadly habits. The better way to build those dopamine highways is through healthy thrill seeking such as sports or other activities that provide the dopamine driven thrill without introducing substances on which your brain will come to rely.

This remodeling process of your brain can lead to important changes in how you function as a teen and can unmask potential problems. A number of mental health challenges like mood difficulties such as depression or bipolar disorder or thinking difficulties like schizophrenia often emerge in the adolescent years. When the teenage brain is under stress, the pruning process can be even more intense and more of the circuits may be diminished and less effective, making teens more vulnerable to brain disorders.[41] Even average pruning can leave a brain unable to keep moods in balance and thoughts coordinated with reality. Drugs and alcohol present a further challenge in that regard. If you think you might be struggling with such issues you need to speak with an adult about it so you can be treated appropriately and get healthy again.

Dr. Siegel identifies four drivers that motivate teens to use drugs and alcohol: experimentation, social connection, self-medication and addiction.[42] The desire for experimentation arises from the low dopamine levels that make teens especially susceptible to wanting to raise them with dopamine enhancing substances. This can also apply to non-dopamine enhancing drugs like LSD and psilocybin where one gets a dopamine thrill from the act of exploration itself. When you do something that could get you in trouble, the rush you feel is from your brain producing dopamine. The social connection driver arises from drugs and alcohol being "social lubricants" that help us open up to others and meet people, like the participants in Plato's *Symposium*. Teens often drink to help them loosen up at a party when they might be otherwise shy and reserved. Of course it is better to overcome those typical insecurities without the crutch of a substance. Self-medication applies to those with disorders who treat themselves either consciously or subconsciously. Depression may drive someone to take amphetamines to get revved up. A bipolar disorder can drive someone to use drugs to modulate their feelings. Schizophrenics may use drugs to quiet the voices and hallucinations that are terrifying them. Self-medication only applies to people with such disorders already present.

Dr. Siegel's fourth driver is addiction, which happens when you need more of a substance to reach your desired state. Your brain and body will develop a tolerance either because your brain is getting used to the presence of certain drugs or your liver is metabolizing a substance more quickly. Heroin addicts commonly report that they are constantly "chasing that first high" and most are content to just forestall the "jones" or withdrawal symptoms. Addicts get so used to the dopamine surge from their limbic region that their cortical region makes decisions by weighing the reward but not the risks from the dangerous behavior. That could mean physically or psychologically dangerous or "getting in trouble" dangerous.

111

Alcoholic teens often engage in binge drinking where large quantities of alcohol are consumed in a single setting. This damages the brain and can lead to blackouts where your limbic memory region, the hippocampus, shuts down so that afterward you simply don't recall what happened to you. You can go on enjoying the party during a blackout but your brain is not making decisions in a normal process. That obviously makes you vulnerable to engage in dangerous behavior. If you have ever been unable to remember everything that happened after a night of drinking, it means you had a blackout and is a warning that you might be an alcoholic.

Teenage brains respond to the introduction of drugs or alcohol with a cascade of behavioral and physiological responses that can bring on an addiction. Altering the neural functioning of our bodies and brains can make the dopamine release dependent on the drug. That means that addicts need a substance to provide what most people get from normal everyday activity. Research has proven that the earlier in adolescence one is introduced to alcohol and drugs, the more likely they are to develop an addiction. It is so much better to postpone such exploration until your brain is more able to handle it.

As advancing science unveils more mysteries about the human brain, genetic research is also in its early stages. Studies suggest some of us could have a gene that triggers our brain's motivational circuitry when we consume a particular substance. Whether it's genetic or not, addicts know that once the trigger occurs, an intense focus of attention, thought, energy and behavior is directed to the substance. Alcohol, cocaine, amphetamines, barbiturates, and opiates can all activate that circuit. Rats given cocaine in studies have chosen that dopamine stimulating drug over food and died of starvation. In humans, the dopamine surge occurs not only after ingesting the substance but also when thinking about it and being around places or people with whom it has been taken. Those people and places become triggers in our brains.

Even if you never get addicted, drugs and alcohol alter your conscious experience of the world and impact how you see reality. Alcohol poisoning has been proven to kill brain cells and their neural connections, especially in regions that control attention and memory. Since the teenage brain is not fully processing all available information, teenagers are more likely to over consume drugs and alcohol. Extreme gluttony can weaken your ability to manage your body, your consciousness can fail to keep you alert. Some substances can even slow your central nervous system down enough to kill you, which is what happens in a fatal drug overdose.

Pearl

That's what happened on October 4, 1970 to Janis Joplin, the first woman lead singer in the previously male dominated world of rock music. As told in her biography *Pearl* by Ellis Amburn, her friends from high school were saddened but not surprised. As a young girl, Janis was driven and overly proud of herself, constantly seeking recognition. Raised in a strict middle class Texas family, she found her love of music at a young age. Joining the church choir in elementary school fulfilled that love and another kind of love too when she met her first boyfriend. She was a bright student in junior high and a clever writer for the school paper but she didn't fully recognize these talents and instead gained a reputation for going out behind the library and making out with boys. As she matured, she focused more on her lack of curves and pretty skin than on her notable qualities. It is so easy, especially for teens, to see only what you don't have and not the gifts you possess. Janis' low self-esteem led to low self-respect, and laziness took over as she let her personal appearance and hygiene deteriorate. By the time she entered Thomas Jefferson High School in Port Arthur, TX in 1956 she had developed her trashy persona accompanied by a foul mouth. It did not bring her many friends and in fact she was shunned by her classmates.

Rejection from her peers led to delinquency which ended up attracting a group of boys who liked her spunkiness. She was like one of the guys, except when she was providing sexual favors to them, which was the characteristic that came to dominate her persona. Feeding her lust was not the only dangerous behavior she engaged in with her friends. They climbed atop a high bridge on one occasion and even got in a couple of car accidents. Once her vehicle flipped over several times but amazingly none of the drunken passengers were injured. By junior year, her brain was maturing and she fell in with a group of musically inclined boys who provided the social life she always craved. They recognized her love and talent for singing and helped her develop it by introducing her to blues singers of the era. You could say she was reaching Aristotle's second level of friendship as she reciprocated her new friends' kindness with sexual favors. She was falling into a party lifestyle of sex and drinking but happiness eluded her.

Her friends graduated a year ahead of Janis leaving her to face pennies thrown at her in the hallway by classmates calling her a cheap whore. She was an oddball for sure, reading the beat poets who became a cultural force years later. A friend who remembers her showing up drunk at graduation said "she broke all of the rules in a redneck town."[43] Janis took social risks with her appearance and behavior and didn't care what all the mean people thought. She rejected them by rejecting the popular racism of the day which brought even more scorn upon her. This was a couple of years after Rosa Parks refused to give up her bus seat, when Martin Luther King Jr had begun trying to convince the good people of Alabama to see their wrongful racist ways. Janis' recognition of emerging art and her embrace of one of history's greatest liberation movements, put her in the vanguard of the Cultural Revolution. She had flaws aplenty but her kindness to the downtrodden persisted as a quality she carried to her death.

According to her biographer, she looked back sadly on her high school years feeling that everyone hated her. Friends confirm that she was widely ridiculed but the inscriptions in her high school yearbook show she had real friends who recognized her true qualities underneath her obvious weaknesses. One boy wrote "You are the nicest hunk of junk in the school but just the sweetest girl."[44] An inscription from "Ace" told her she was boy crazy and should cool it.[45] Despite her shortcomings, she was diligent in learning about the music she loved and other forms of self-exploration like writing and painting. She became a fan of Bessie Smith, a blues singer who died destitute. Years later Janis would provide a proper gravestone for Bessie's final resting place.

THINK: Have you ever felt like an outcast at school?

Senior year brought her first lesbian experience leading to a life engaging in wild sexual exploits of all sorts but always shunning true love. Later in her career she told an audience that she had slept with 2,000 men, more or less, "and a few hundred chicks."[46] The Sixties Cultural Revolution had arrived, when it seemed like everyone was making the easy choices. The party life never brought Janis happiness. Instead she became lost in a constant fog unable to recognize her great talents.

Entering a local university in 1960 she joined the burgeoning protest movement by conducting the school's first "sit-in" defending a group of Puerto Rican students. This was a form of protest that became very popular in those times. Still trying to find herself, she tried painting. A mentor said she "had heart and passion but no skill."[47] Janis possessed the important qualities but never chose to develop the necessary skills. She did develop her talent for singing but always needed alcohol to overcome her stage fright, even after being treated for alcoholism at age 17.

She eventually enrolled in the University of Texas at Austin in 1962 where her friends among the music crowd cultivated her musical development and ultimately arranged for her to try out professionally in San Francisco. She was a big hit and was able to provide opportunities for her friends just as they provided opportunities for her. The California music scene also introduced drugs into the intensifying party habits that came to define Janis' persona. She was gaining popularity but always blowing big opportunities by getting in fights or getting injured from her dangerous lifestyle. Singing provided a livelihood but all the money went to drugs. She was having so much fun that she forgot that she went to San Francisco to become a singer. Singing began to interfere with her partying. Her self-destructive personality was taking its toll by 1965 when she was so emaciated that she tried to commit herself to San Francisco General Hospital. They rejected her as a derelict trying to freeload.

Friends threw her a party to raise bus fare so she could go home to Texas and try to get healthy again. She had a new boyfriend at the party and instead of going back to Texas, she went to Seattle with him. Before long, the drugs took their toll on her boyfriend who had to be hospitalized with severe hallucinations. Janis went back to Port Arthur and her boyfriend showed up later to ask her father if he could marry her. With her father's consent, the wedding was planned but the groom got cold feet and stood Janis up. She had hit rock bottom. At the age of 22, she knew it was time to clean up and get her life back on track. She enrolled in community college and avoided drinking and drugs. She kept herself neat although classmates described her as irritable and nasty. Fearing the drug culture, she was reluctant to follow her old friends' advice to get back into music. She recognized its power over her. However, her love of music was overwhelming, it defined her. She returned to San Francisco and became more popular than before.

Janis knew herself, her fears were well founded as alcohol and drugs gradually came back into her life. She managed it all better than earlier years but was still a slave to her addictions. Old friendships faded as she developed into a major star. She was too proud to appreciate the help she was given, leaving behind those who loved her, and not just her fiancé. Her first hit song, *Bye Bye Baby,* was written by one of her Texas friends but she never gave him credit. It didn't matter to her as she became the most famous woman in music as the seminal year of 1967 got underway.

January 14, 1967 was the date of the Human Be-In in San Francisco's Golden Gate Park and Janis Joplin enthralled the audience with her wild blues rock singing. That was the event where Timothy Leary coined "Turn on, tune in, drop out." Later that year, the Monterey Pop festival became the most famous rock concert ever and again Janis was one of the stars of the show. The other big star at Monterey was a young black guitar player named Jimi Hendrix who was making it big in Great Britain. Janis and Jimi hit it off and she saw having an affair with a black man as a good way to give the finger to the racists back home.

Like Janis, Jimi found his love for music at a young age. Too poor to afford a guitar, he carried around a broomstick and pretended to play Elvis Presley songs. The son of alcoholic parents, Jimi's father did not take his sons to their mother's funeral after drinking had killed her. Instead he gave them each a shot of whiskey and said that's how men deal with loss. Soon after his mother's death, the 15 year old managed to save $5 for a guitar and went on to win talent contests. By 1969, Jimi Hendrix had become the world's highest paid rock star at 26 years old. Whether he had the alcoholic gene or it was just environmental influences, Jimi would struggle with alcohol for his entire young adult life. He told a journalist that he could not handle hard liquor which set off a bottled up anger, a destructive fury he almost never displayed otherwise. He and Janis always remained dear friends but his drunken violence kept her at a distance.

Janis was such a big star in 1967 that she was being described as a female Jim Morrison, which inevitably brought him into her life. He was a spectator at the Human Be-In and was envious of those who got to perform even though he and The Doors had the number one single with *Light My Fire*. He wanted to meet Janis and she had sex with him like she had sex with everybody, but they didn't hit it off. They were both known for their monstrous egos and often fought with one another over the following years.

Like Janis and Jimi, Jim Morrison found his talent at a young age. An avid reader of history, philosophy and the beat poets, Jim took a strong liking to Friedrich Nietzsche. He read such obscure books that his high school teachers had to verify that they really existed. Growing up the son of a Navy captain in an easy going home, as long as everyone obeyed Dad's rules, his siblings saw him as a near genius. While he always thought he would be a writer, he never expected to become a singer. That came about after he showed his poetry to a friend who thought his words would make good song lyrics, so he and Ray Manzarek formed the Doors. In college, he had a falling out with his parents after he toured the aircraft carrier that his father captained in the Vietnam War. He was appalled that one man could have such power over life and death on such a huge scale. His mother came to one of his concerts years later and left in tears after Jim refused to see her. Mothers always love their children, and she continued to clip every one of his newspaper articles. His brother Andy said they remained proud of Jim.

Jim spent most of his adult life with his girlfriend, Pamela Courson but became known as a notorious womanizer. Having become an international sex symbol with his iconic leather pants, all the Doors concerts were attended by young women known as groupies whose highest aspirations were to have sex with Jim. He was the quintessential rock star who could have just about any woman he wanted. Cavorting with a young groupie backstage before one of his concerts in 1967, Jim was sprayed with mace by a New Haven, CT police officer. He proceeded to take the stage and launched into a profanity laced tirade that got him arrested and sparked riots in the area.

Not all of those newspaper clippings made his mother proud as Jim got a reputation as an out of control drunk getting into trouble with the police. This is another trait he shared with Janis although they were always antagonists to each other. One spring night in 1968 at a New York nightclub, Jimi Hendrix was performing and a drunken Jim Morrison joined him on stage. As Hendrix played guitar, Morrison attempted to unbutton his pants and simulate oral

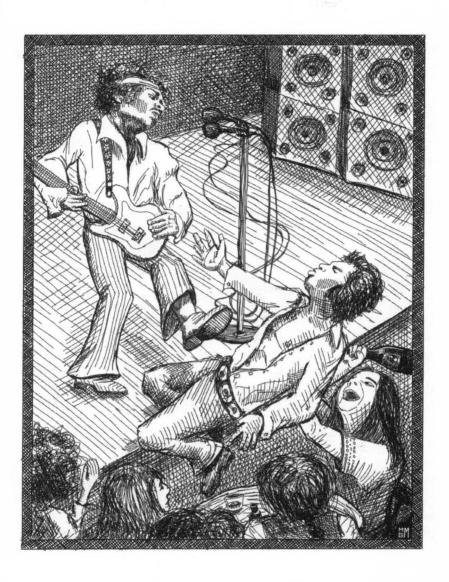

THINK: Do you think Janis, Jimi and Jim were having
fun or running from their demons?

sex. Jimi pushed him away and Morrison fell into the front table where Janis was sitting. Just as annoyed at him as Jimi was, she smashed a bottle over his head. All three rock stars were near their 25th birthday and spiraling out of control.

In 1970, Janis went back to Texas for her 10th high school reunion and thought she would create quite a stir being such a big star. The event turned out to be a bore. The trip did provide her an opportunity to make peace with her family and she returned to California in a better state of mind. She asked her lawyer to rewrite her will to include all the family members that she had previously written out. She also set aside $2,500 for a gathering of her friends after her death. It is not that she felt the end was near. She had been working with the Doors' producer on her latest record. Her friends told how excited she was about the single *Me and Bobby McGee* written by her friend Kris Kristofferson. Things seemed to be going very well for Janis at that point. It was around then that Jim Morrison reached out to her. He was getting ready to move to Paris and wanted to make peace with his old drinking buddy. Jim was trying to get his drinking under control and did not look good. Friends said it was a warm visit.

In the fall of 1970 Jimi Hendrix was touring Europe but he and the band were too drunk and drugged up to entertain the fans who booed them on several occasions. A couple of days after a concert in London, Jimi's girlfriend found him unconscious and called for help which did not arrive in time. He had passed out drunk. The prefrontal region of his brain was no longer able to carry out its coordination and balance the streams of information from his body and the outside world. He lost control of his basic bodily functions and choked on his own vomit. Jimi Hendrix was pronounced dead on September 18, 1970 at the age of 27. That is the same age at which Brian Jones of the Rolling Stones died a year earlier in what the coroner then reported as "death by misadventure," noting Jones' liver and heart were heavily enlarged by drug and alcohol abuse. When Janis' publicist called her to see if she had any comment, she replied "I wonder what they'll say about me when I die."[48] She didn't go to Jimi's funeral in his hometown of Seattle and instead went to her lawyer's office to sign the will they recently rewrote.

A couple of weeks later on October 4, 1970 Janis didn't show up at a recording session. Seeing her car parked in front of her hotel, a friend found her dead in her room from a heroin overdose, she was also 27 years old. She had only recently resumed taking the drug after a long hiatus but received a fatal dose from her dealer who also lost some other customers that week; street drugs obviously do not go through any quality control procedures. Narcotics like heroin slow the activity of the central nervous system, which includes respiratory and cardiovascular systems. In an overdose situation, insufficient oxygen gets delivered to the brain and the body shuts down. Janis had lived the life of a true Hedonist but did not live to see her song *Me and Bobby McGee* reach number one on the U.S. singles chart with its iconic line "Freedom's just another word for nothing left to lose." The invitation to Janis Joplin's memorial read that music would be provided by the Grateful Dead and "Drinks are on Pearl."

On hearing of Janis Joplin's death, Jim Morrison said "You're drinking with number three."[49] He was found dead in a Paris bathtub the following July, also at age 27. No autopsy was performed but his girlfriend Pamela died weeks later from a heroin overdose. A couple of years later on March 8, 1973 Janis' dear friend, Ron "Pigpen" McKernan of the Grateful Dead, died from the ravages of alcohol poisoning, he too was 27. A couple of decades later, a child of that seminal year of 1967, Nirvana's Kurt Cobain was found dead in his mansion from suicide. It was April 5, 1994 and his mother told a reporter "Now he's gone and joined that stupid club. I told him not to join that stupid club."[50] He was not the last, Amy Winehouse also succumbed to alcohol poisoning on July 23, 2011 at the same age of 27. A Wikipedia search of "27 Club" shows dozens of popular musicians who met their death at that age since the beginning of the 20th century. Some of them resulted from accidents like a plane crash or illnesses like cancer but most are related to drug and alcohol abuse which usually began in their teenage years.

Who's Doing It

There was a precipitous drop in heroin use immediately following Janis Joplin's death but the drug culture in America was still a few years away from peaking. Monitoring The Future (MTF) is a research project at the University of Michigan that has been interviewing young Americans since 1975 with detailed questions regarding their drug use. In 1991 their population was expanded to include 8th and 10th graders and their 50,000 interviews each year make it one of the most relied-upon scientific sources of information on trends in legal and illicit drug use by American adolescents. Their reports are available online at www.monitoringthefuture.org.

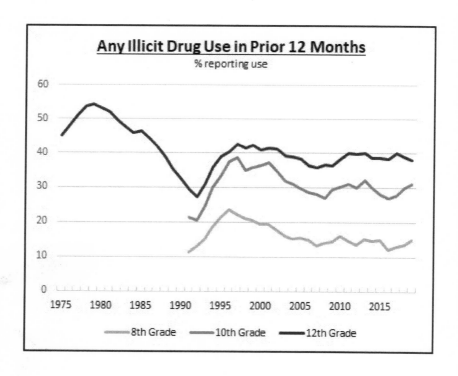

The chart above shows the peak on the dark line representing 12th graders reporting use of any illicit substance in the prior twelve months. That was the 1979 survey in which 54.2% of those questioned said they had used any of a wide array of illicit drugs, marijuana being the most common. By then the dangers of drugs were becoming obvious and the line dropped below 50% in 1982 on the way to bottoming at 27% in 1992. Never since have more than half of 12th graders reported having used illicit drugs in the past year, although in a separate series of interviews a slim majority in recent years report use sometime in their life. The interviews include questions about perceived risks and social acceptance of each drug and the data conclusively show those two factors to be important determinants of the level of drug use. Not only were the risks of the Sixties Counterculture lifestyle clearly perceptible by the Eighties, but social acceptance declined along with a major campaign led by First Lady Nancy Reagan exhorting teens to "Just say no."

The responses to questions on alcohol use show a more persistent decline with response rates currently near all-time lows, although more people continue to answer affirmatively to having used alcohol or gotten drunk than those having used drugs. The decline masks a dangerous acceptance of getting drunk among some teens whose brains can least handle it; but now that you possess knowledge about modern brain science, you know better.

The early Nineties saw a reversal in the decade long trend of reduced drug use. Obvious lessons from "unfortunate role models" of the drug counterculture were fading from memory and the researchers note that news coverage of the drug issue plummeted between 1989 and 1993. You can see the lines moving up and down in a range since then with an uptrend emerging in the last few years. MTF attributes the increase to recent marijuana legalization initiatives which have led to decreases in perceived risks and increased social acceptance. As with alcohol, the percentages using illicit drugs other than marijuana are near all-time lows so the uptick is attributable to marijuana. Smoking pot may be somewhat benign to a mature brain, and society may now be accepting its use, but that does not mean it is safe for a teenage brain undergoing the remodeling process.

Almost like an alcohol blackout, the active component of marijuana, Tetrahydrocannabinol or THC, suppresses the activity of the neurons in the hippocampus (under your knuckles on either side in the hand model) which is largely responsible for learning and memory.[51] Studies have proven that learned behaviors that depend on the hippocampus deteriorate after substantial marijuana use. This is especially critical to adolescents not only for the reasons regarding the permanent effects it can have on their brains but the need for high school students to be able to recall for tests and other school requirements. Cannabis consumption undoubtedly puts you at a disadvantage to get better grades than your classmates. Teachers and counselors at your school can confirm that there is a distinct pattern of declining grades among students who take up marijuana in high school. Don't fool yourself, they know who is smoking and vaping. It may not impair your coordination like alcohol does but it does impair your judgment and perception. Science is also disproving the myth that pot is not addictive. Although probably not physically addictive like opiates, common withdrawal symptoms experienced by pot smokers trying to quit include irritability, insomnia, sweating and gastrointestinal problems. If you are among the one out of six eighth graders who have tried pot, be careful not to turn into the one out fifteen who smoke it daily by twelfth grade, a clear sign of addiction.

It is likely that you will have tried alcohol and marijuana before you graduate high school. Far less likely that you will have tried any other drugs; less than 20% of twelfth graders had in 2019. Use of more dangerous drugs like hallucinogens, ecstasy and others are reported by less than 5% of respondents. Studies have found that ecstasy users' brains showed a significant reduction in serotonin transporters that seem to be a long term or permanent effect, resulting in loss of both verbal and visual short term memory. Before you might experiment with a substance, take great care to understand the distinct risks to you as a teenager. It is far better to be patient and hold off on such exploration until your brain is better equipped to handle it. Addictions do not announce themselves and most of those people in the 27 Club were able to handle it in their teen years and went on to develop their talents. It was only later that they realized the deadly monkey on their back.

THINK: Do you want to try alcohol or drugs?

There are various reasons why you might try alcohol or drugs; curiosity or peer pressure, or even peer acceptance. If your friend does it, it seems OK. Drugs can provide a euphoria that can make you at peace with a world that is otherwise troubling you. However, you need to intuitively know that those troubles will only accumulate in your absence from reality. Dr. Siegel says that teens can be too rational in looking only at the reward and need to concentrate on incorporating their intuitive gut feelings and heartfelt sensations.[52] Think thoroughly about what you do and listen to your conscience.

Experiencing life from such a thoughtful standpoint is not about suppressing relatively benign impulses like driving fast or eating junk food. It is about embracing positive goals that are intuitively important to you. Having a goal to stay in shape will keep the junk food to a minimum and paying for your own car insurance will keep you driving within the law. Both are examples of ways to build that stronger foundation for your life, making you a better person in the long run.

Whatever their motivation, MTF says American high school students show a level of involvement with illicit drugs that is among the highest in the world's industrialized nations. Even by longer term historical standards, current rates in the U.S. remain extremely high, though generally not as high as in the peak years of the 1970s drug epidemic. Dr. Siegel says that addictive behaviors, like shopping or gambling, also involve the reward circuit's major transmitter, dopamine. He says a better way to generate high dopamine levels is to work hard at something and finish it. The disciplined effort will be rewarded not with a dopamine surge but a gradual rise, providing a feeling of deep satisfaction.[53] Drugs will never provide deep satisfaction. They will only provide a transitory self-centered experience loaded with dangerous risks and a constant yearning for more.

Focusing instead on building your talents strengthens your self-esteem and prepares you to contribute to society. Having a healthy brain is vital to realizing your potential. The Roman poet Juvenal, famous for his satire and the root of the word meaning to act foolishly, was the first to say we "should pray for a sound mind in a sound body." Ever since he wrote that in the 1st century, the mind body balance has been recognized as integral to living a full life. We know how to keep a healthy body and modern science has found ways we can cultivate the growth of our brains' interactive fibers of the prefrontal cortex, the executive region. Engaging in positive interactions with others, such as joining groups, is one way. Intellectual conversation gets the brain's synapses working across all those areas represented on your hand model as well as the cerebellum. Another way to build those neural highways is through self-reflection. Thinking about your own personal strengths and weaknesses and the goals you want to achieve. It is one more example of modern science confirming the ancient oracle's admonition to "Know Thyself."

Chapter 5: Rock...

*Do not be bound by limits you place on yourself.
It is only when you reach beyond what you think
you can do that you will almost surely do far
more than you thought you could*

-   Tecumseh

As Pucksinwah turned over the final chunk of burnt wood in the fire, Chiksika threw off his blanket saying "I'll put on some more wood, Father." The family had come along with their tribe of Shawnees to a Grand Council of eight major Indian nations to form a trading alliance with the British. They would agree to cease all raids against settlers coming across the Appalachian Mountains but the British had to enforce a ban on them from doing so.

The 15 years prior to 1768 had been marked by increasing tensions on the then western frontier of Pennsylvania and Ohio among the Native Americans and the white settlers from Europe. The original traders were welcomed as a way for the tribes to exchange their furs and pelts for all the wonderful products from the old world. The traders became close friends with the natives who liked to play the French against the British for better terms of trade. That fed the already existing enmity between the two dominant European powers who would wage proxy battles in the New World of North America by pitting the Indian tribes against one another. A key moment came when the British were attempting to build a fort at the confluence of the Allegheny and Monongahela rivers, the forks of the Ohio River. French forces, aided by Shawnee warriors, seized the site from the British troops commanded by 22 year old Lieutenant Colonel George Washington, and named it Fort Duquesne (pronounced Du-Kane).

Washington was fighting on behalf of King George III who found his empire enmeshed in a world at war. Great Britain's Seven Years War spread over five continents with the French and Indian War being the North American component. It lasted from the battle of Fort Duquesne in 1754 until Great Britain and France made peace in 1763.

Washington was the senior American aide to British General Edward Braddock in his disastrous attempt to retake the fort and expel the French from the area. Pucksinwah was a warrior chief in the French defense that ambushed Washington's army. After being surprised by Shawnee and French fighters shooting muskets from the trees, the intrepid Washington rode back and forth across the battlefield rallying the outnumbered British and Virginian forces into an organized retreat. He was allowed to peacefully bring his troops back to Virginia. Historians point to the battle as an example of the young Washington's initiative and bravery but also his inexperience and impulsiveness.

Fighting under George Washington as a wagoner transporting supplies, was another young man named Daniel Boone who was raised on the western frontiers of Pennsylvania and North Carolina. Both men had similar experiences losing their fathers at a young age. Neither man was especially religious but each kept certain precepts close to their hearts. It was their way of building guardrails around their lives to keep them on the right and good path. Washington went on to purchase land from various Indian tribes becoming a successful land speculator before leading the Revolutionary War and becoming the father of his country. Daniel Boone also speculated in land, unsuccessfully, and he too became a leader of the people who knew him best, through diligent work and always respecting others. Fort Duquesne was retaken by British forces in 1758 and renamed Fort Pitt, known today as Pittsburgh, Pennsylvania.

Pucksinwah saw the British victory at Ft. Pitt as a premonition of a wider British victory in the French and Indian War. His Shawnee people had always been valiant warriors in the battles that came to define land boundaries between the numerous Indian nations. Unlike virtually all the other tribes, who sank their roots in a specified territory and remained there, the Shawnees were nomadic. They finally got permanent land in Ohio and the first Shawnee born on it was Pucksinwah. While they welcomed traders, they did not welcome the surveyors and settlers who followed. Pucksinwah led frequent raids on forts in the area, burning structures and destroying crops and livestock in an effort to drive the settlers back east. The situation got so bad that King George issued that proclamation in 1763 prohibiting everyone but traders from traveling west of the Appalachian Mountains. This incensed people like George Washington who lost all their land rights in the area.

Despite the proclamation, a steady stream of immigrants to the New World were coming over the mountains and traveling west until they found their place to settle. The settlers were not only risking being in violation of the King's proclamation, they were also risking their lives competing for the resources of the rich land with the natives who lived there. As a warrior chief, Pucksinwah's opinion was important to the Grand Council deciding whether to enter into an expanded trade treaty with the British. The Shawnees didn't like the white man coming into their land, but like all their neighboring tribes, they had become very dependent on trade. King George did indeed prevail in the French and Indian War as he prevailed around the world, cementing Great Britain as the world's dominant superpower on this March night in 1768.

As Chiksika got up for more firewood, he and Pucksinwah were suddenly illuminated in a greenish light. They both spun towards the source in time to see a brilliant meteor streak across the heavens from the north, lasting a full twenty seconds. It was an awesome spectacle whose silent majesty was punctuated by the wail of a baby's cry. As the warriors sat stunned, one of the aunts came out of the shelter to tell Pucksinwah he had a son.

The meteor was seen by tribes as far north as today's Quebec and as far south as Memphis. A few minutes passed before Pucksinwah entered the shelter to see his wife under a deerskin holding their infant asleep in the crook of her arm. His body glistened from being rubbed with a protective coating of bear oil. Indian babies were typically not named for a couple of weeks until Moneto, the Great Spirit, sent a sign of what the baby should be called. In this case there was no need to wait. Pucksinwah told his wife of the Great Panther Passing Across, whose Indian word is Tecumseh.

> **THINK: What does your name mean to your family?**

The Shawnees were very diligent about recording their history which has been archived in hundreds of volumes as the Draper Papers, housed at the Wisconsin Historical Society. We can thank Allan W. Eckert, a novelist and historian of the American frontier for interpreting that written record over a multi-decade career culminating in his masterful 1992 book *A Sorrow in Our Heart: The Life of Tecumseh*. In what the author calls a *narrative biography*, he reconstructs dialogue from the detailed historical record and presents his subjects with the fullness of characters in a novel. Most of the quotes presented here come from that work and I have footnoted the more important ones. Matching the historical record with the perspective of the frontier settlers, we are fortunate to have *Daniel Boone Master of the Wilderness*, the authoritative biography written in 1939 by John Bakeless. He also painstakingly investigated the historical record in order to confirm only what he positively could about a storied American character. Both books confirm each other's versions of some incredible events that defined the early United States of America. The history of the American frontier is rich with lessons on humanity that span these extremely diverse cultures. We'll see how we all have so much in common too.

Tecumseh was born into an era when his culture was under assault by the assimilation of the steady stream of settlers pushing the American frontier further west. Later that year, an amalgamation of New York tribes named the Iroquois sold The

Kan-tuck-kee territory to the British for £10,000 but never told the Shawnees about selling their favorite hunting grounds across the Ohio River. The Iroquois had a reputation for shady dealings including selling land belonging to other tribes. It was a time when tribes throughout the eastern half of the continent were busy making deals with land developers and settlers. The most famous settler was Daniel Boone who was well known and liked among the Cherokee tribes to the south. Boone was always better at the settling part than the speculating part as most of his land ventures went bust, and not always because of Indian attacks. He learned about the area's rich hunting grounds when he was fighting for George Washington in the Braddock expedition to save Ft. Pitt. He had been supporting his growing family since then primarily by hunting and trapping for furs, of which he saw plenty in the Kan-tuck-kee hunting grounds. In light of the deal signed between the Iroquois and King George, Boone thought it would be an opportune time to make a settlement there.

Dec 22, 1769 was his first attack by a Shawnee hunting party led by a chief with considerable knowledge of the whites who nicknamed him Captain Will. Boone may have been familiar with him from his days growing up on the Pennsylvania frontier before his family moved to North Carolina. He and his partner had lost the skins they had acquired trapping in the wilderness and other belongings on this early expedition to Kentucky. Boone had staked everything he had, and seven months of hard work, which all came to naught. It could have been worse though; many other intruders into the then western wilderness were killed by Indians who sold their scalps to either the French or British, depending on who was paying more. The Shawnees had yet to see white men in these hunting grounds and they told Boone that the wild game there was the Indians' cattle and killing it was downright theft.

Boone and his partner were held by the Shawnees and released after seven days. They lost all their belongings but were provided with moccasins, a doeskin or patch-leather, a small gun and enough gunpowder and lead shot to kill food for themselves on the way back to the Virginia settlements to the southeast. Captain

Will warned "if you are foolish as to venture here again you may be sure the wasps and yellow jackets will sting you severely." Boone later dreamt of that happening which he interpreted as a premonition that he would be wounded by Indians. The creek in Kentucky where he slept is still called Dreaming Creek. Despite Boone's fears, he had no intention of staying away.

The two hunters shook hands with the Shawnees and left, or so the Indians thought. Boone and his partner followed them and snuck into their camp at night to retrieve their horses and other belongings. They were caught again but escaped and hid in the wilderness. Captain Will was not to be made a fool and was determined to capture them, but Boone amazed the natives by his woodsman skills. He eluded his pursuers over several months by living in caves and shooting at them from phenomenally long distances. His partner was eventually killed and by the end of his two year trip Boone had little to show for his considerable efforts except a thorough knowledge of Kentucky.

Tecumseh was also learning about the Kentucky hunting lands across the river where his father and brother would go for long stretches. He had always been a quiet baby which was very important to the Indians. Not only could noise scare off game they were hunting but it could also alert enemies to their whereabouts. By the time he was three years old, Tecumseh was known as an especially quiet, good natured boy among the many friends he had to play with in the tribe. He had proven to be talented with his makeshift bow and arrows. During one of his father's journeys, his mother gave birth to triplets. That brought Pucksinwah great pride but the Shawnee prophet and medicine man saw the rare event as foreboding disaster for the tribe. The youngest of the triplets was almost the opposite of Tecumseh. He would scream and cry without reason so he was given the name Lowawluwaysica (pronounced Low-WAH-loo-WAY-sik-ah) – He Makes Loud Noise.

By the age of six, Tecumseh was the best among all the kids, even older ones, at the various games they played. He was always picked as the "captain" of any team. Uncommonly skilled at the bow and arrows he made, when he would set out into the woods to hunt, he would return with his buckskin pouch filled with squirrels, rabbits, quail or turkeys that he shot. He used remarkable stealth and tracking ability that years later would make him a great warrior. His father, uncles and other tribesmen taught him other essential skills, like hand to hand combat and dressing battlefield wounds with whatever nature provided. Pucksinwah also taught him the strategy of warfare, how to outthink an enemy and keep him confused but to never underestimate a foe.

Pucksinwah also taught Tecumseh about Moneto, the Supreme Being of all things, who dispenses His blessings on those who earn His good will, while bringing unspeakable sorrow to those whose conduct displeases Him. "No one is forced to believe in these matters" the father told his son. "Force is not necessary. We know them to be the truth. Morality is a fixed law, but each of us must be his own judge." Puksinwah was telling Tecumseh about setting his own personal guardrails. Calling morality fixed means there is a distinct right and wrong that we must each judge for ourselves. Pucksinwah went on to describe a morality of being true to yourself and not to worry what others think. The foundation of Shawnee morality could be summed up as love your neighbor as yourself because Moneto loves him as He loves you. Notice how people from a culture totally distinct from western civilization held such familiar views.

By this time, George Washington was a wealthy land speculator who the Iroquois chief bitterly referred to as "Town Destroyer." Chief Red Jacket was watching the whites buy land encircling his people, who were gradually mixing into white society. It wasn't just the Indian villages that were disappearing but the culture too as the settlers' lifestyle proved to be more comfortable. The Indians knew all too well that the tomahawk marks the surveyors made on the trees meant many more whites would be following. Boone came back with his wife Rebecca and ten children in September 1773 and it is said that Rebecca and daughter Jemima were the first white women to stand on the banks of the Kentucky River. Public records show his grandson Enoch was the first white male born in Kentucky.

Soon after they arrived, his son James and another boy went out with a hunting party from the settlement. Asleep in their camp, a group of Indians came upon them in a pre-dawn raid shooting James and his friend. Another member of the party hid beneath a pile of driftwood in the river and witnessed the wounded boys being brutally tortured. They knew the leader as Big Jim who had often visited Boone's cabin, but their friend showed no mercy. James begged to be put out of his misery with a quick tomahawk blow to the head but he was refused before being burned to death. The witness' account caused such a sensation that the governor of Virginia got the Cherokee chiefs to hold someone responsible and two braves were executed, but not Big Jim. A friend of Boone's saw a group of peaceful Cherokees who had nothing to do with the killings and killed them in retaliation, almost sparking a war. That would come soon enough.

In May 1774, Boone went back to visit his son's grave and described the melancholy as the worst of his life. He was feeling the sting of the Indian wasps and yellow jackets for sure and the swarms were gathering. Kentucky was getting hot after an Indian friend of most white men was lured into a trap and his family was murdered by a settler. Tahgahute had taken the white name Logan and the murder of his family set off Lord Dunmore's War that raged along several hundred miles of frontier in the summer and early autumn of 1774. Lieutenant Boone and a friend were sent out among the surveyors to warn them of the hostilities. They accomplished their task in scant time, earning Boone a promotion to Captain in the militia and command of three forts. His commander reported for his record that: "Mr. Boone is very diligent at Castle's woods and keeps up good order."[54] It was clear that Captain Boone had used his formative years to build a rock solid foundation for his life.

King George III was sensing the colonists were getting ready to declare independence and he wanted the Shawnees and surrounding tribes to ally with him against the rebellious states as they called themselves. At the seminal battle of Point Pleasant, hundreds of Indians and state militia confronted one another in a fierce battle that began with gunshot and arrow volleys from side to side. When ammunition ran out, both sides came together in vicious hand to hand combat. The Indians were led by the Shawnees whose style in war was to shriek and scream to instill fear and confusion. The latter was abundant as each side attacked the other with knives and tomahawks. Bloody hours passed from when the sun was at its highest until the harvest point. As the ground became muddy with blood, each side hoped they could hold on until darkness would bring a lull.

Chiksika fought courageously in his first major battle, swinging his war club with fierce accuracy against the militiamen converging around him. He felt great pride when he noticed his father watching him approvingly. When the warriors killed a settler they would scalp them by cutting off a wide strip of their skin from their forehead to the back of their neck and save the bloody scalp in their pouch. The British in Detroit would pay $50 per scalp and $100 per prisoner at that time. The hair on the scalps indicated if men, women or children had been killed.

Keeping close to his father as the battle raged, Chiksika watched a lead shot the size of a grape hit his father's chest, slamming him to the ground. Pucksinwah knew the wound was fatal and begged Chiksika to promise him two things. "What, Father? Anything! Promise you what?" The dying war chief said "Promise me you will take care of Tecumseh... teach him to be a good warrior... a good man. Guide him in the right way."[55] He asked Chiksika to do the same with the rest of the family and provide for them. Chiksika promised he would. The second promise was to never make peace with the white man.

THINK: Have you lost a loved one yet?

The battle ended before sunset when the Indians retreated after their scouts reported several hundred reinforcements coming to help the settlers. It marked the end of Lord Dunmore's War and the peace established an agreement that the settlers would stay on the Kentucky side of the Ohio River. The Shawnees went back to Ohio angry in defeat. Chiksika rode all the way home supporting Pucksinwah's body propped upright on his horse. He did indeed provide for his brothers and sisters and he taught Tecumseh everything that he had learned. Just as George Washington and Daniel Boone had surrogates to help them through the crisis of losing their fathers, so too did Tecumseh have a fine surrogate in his older brother Chiksika. In her despair, their mother left to join her native tribe of Cherokees to the southwest where it was peaceful. Tecumseh's older sister, Tecumapese, took over the maternal role in the family. Captain Daniel Boone was discharged from the militia and went back to North Carolina to pursue land ventures.

The New New World

Boone found enough investors who saw the peace treaty following the battle of Point Pleasant as providing another opportunity to acquire prime land. He convinced more than 1,000 influential Cherokees, including a key negotiating chief, to join a treaty. At the signing, the Indians had their own attorney and the signature of "Thomas Price, Linguist" guaranteed the accuracy of translation. The Cherokees were happy to sell the land and not just because the white men got them drunk like they so often did with Indians signing land treaties. The Cherokees feared the Shawnees as much as the whites did. They told Boone "there is a dark cloud over that country." Boone expected that the treaty would forestall any trouble and went back to Kentucky with a group of settlers in 1775. He had to get away from North Carolina as creditors were coming after him. A warrant for his arrest for nonpayment of debts read "Gone to Kentucky."

Boone and the settlers travelled through the Cumberland Gap of the Appalachian Mountains from Virginia into Kentucky. After Indian attacks on several camps, the settlers were hard at work in the spring of 1775 building Fort Boonesborough near a big salt lick that attracted a lot of wildlife. The springs were called licks because animals would come to lick the salt seepage from the prehistoric seabed in the limestone country. One lick called "Big Bone Lick" took its name from skeletal remains of huge mammoths and mastodons that died there thousands of years before, caught in the marshy land in which their gigantic bodies would easily sink. So many had perished that one could walk from bone to bone and never touch the ground for several hundred yards. Such was life on the unspoiled frontier where incredible discoveries were commonplace. The huge vertebrae made comfortable camp seats as they were neatly rounded to accommodate a human frame weary from a day of hunting. Boone's biographer, John Bakeless, wrote that the settlers used the bones without troubling themselves much about fossil lore but a few were sent "back to Virginia for the edification of the philosophic Mr. Jefferson."[56] Thomas Jefferson was president of the American Philosophical Society before he was president of the United States of America. While proving Plato's ideal to be governed by philosophers, Jefferson espoused more of the Aristotelian type of philosophy focused on science and empirical observation rather than metaphysical theory.

The settlers had come to establish the Henderson Land Company which would form the basis for the hopeful state of Transylvania. Many of the original settlers went back after facing Indian attacks but for those who remained, two acre lots were apportioned after some contentiousness regarding locations was eventually overcome. The settlers met beneath a huge elm tree to set up rules and legal conventions. Boone got a bill passed "for preserving game" requiring that when game is shot the full animal must be used. He respected the Indians' major complaint that settlers would waste the livestock they killed. Many times, buffalo would lay slain with only their tongues removed and the rest of the meat spoiled. It wasn't pure altruism however, he was also finding he had to travel farther to hunt as the local game was getting depleted. Another Boone bill "for improving the breed of horses" is the forerunner to the State of Kentucky leading the world in horse breeding today. Although he was always diligent, patient and kind, Boone's lifestyle may have conditioned his brain to crave ever more risk. He not only took on great risk of physical danger, he was also too familiar with the hard side of financial risk. Unfortunately the Revolutionary War voided the Transylvania land scheme and Boone lost all his claims. He desperately tried to get recognized as a colony by both the Continental Congress and King George. The political situation in 1775 was confusing, the Declaration of Independence was still months in the future and the colonists did not yet know if they were fighting for rights as British citizens or founding a new republic. He received no positive response from either but the settlement of Kentucky was well underway.

By eight years old, Tecumseh excelled so much in sports that it wasn't even a contest when competing against his own age, he would usually compete with those three or four years older. Mentally he was just as excellent. He constantly probed the tribe's elders for information, showing respect not just to them but concern and compassion to his peers. He had every reason to be proud but was always humble. Through diligent practice he became an expert marksman, he was by far the best hunter. He taught himself to load and fire on the run like he heard Daniel Boone could do. He tried to anyway; it was not easy with the flintlock muskets of those days. Chief Blackfish would spend long hours with the boy explaining politics and policies of the tribe. Tecumapese taught him good character and high morals. One of the more important values she instilled in him was the value of patience. Chiksika taught him the great need for self-control, how not to be ruled by his passions. Tecumseh took these lessons to heart as he built his own rock solid foundation for his life. It had to be a strong foundation since it would be forever burdened by his anger towards the white settlers.

> **THINK: What do you excel at?**

In the summer of 1776 the British and their Indian allies were trying to make life hopeless for the settlers. Boone's daughter Jemima and two other teenage girls were abducted by a war party who silenced them by brandishing their knives and tomahawks. They were bringing the girls back to the Shawnee towns in Ohio when Jemima recognized the chief and told him who she was. He asked if the others were her sisters, she lied and said yes. Hanging Maw was amused, for rare is the Indian that got the better of "Wide Mouth."[57] An hour or two on their trail, Daniel Boone and a group of settlers tracked the war party. Following heal marks in the mud and broken twigs left by the girls, they came across a freshly killed and cut buffalo. Boone correctly predicted they would find the Indians at the next river crossing.

After darkness fell, one of the girls was watching her captor put buffalo meat on a broiling stick when suddenly she saw blood spurt out of his chest amid a sputter of gunshots. "That's Daddy" cried Jemima. "Run gals run!" yelled the rescuers. At least one of the war party was killed and legend says it was Blackfish's son. Boone's party and the girls were all safe. James Fenimore Cooper memorialized the rescue in an episode of his book *The Last of the Mohicans*.

It wasn't long before news from the east reached the settlements reporting that the colonies declared independence and Kentucky was part of it. Fresh stocks of gunpowder and lead shot arrived at Boonesborough in September 1776 to fight the western front of the Revolutionary War.

The year of the three sevens was an active one for Shawnee raids led by Chief Blackfish who came to share mutual respect with Boone. On the morning of April 24th, some of the animals refused to go out of the fort to graze, raising suspicions that there could be Indians in the area. When two men went outside they were attacked and the noise brought Boone and about a dozen others to their aid, which brought the Indians out of the woods. "Boys, we have to fight!" exclaimed Boone "Sell your lives as dear as possible."[58] Savage hand to hand combat ensued with clubbed rifles against knives and tomahawks. Boone went down with a broken ankle and he was about to be scalped when his young friend, Simon Kenton, shot his attacker at close range. Kenton saved Boone three times in that one battle, and like Boone, went on to hold legendary status among the Shawnees.

Tecumseh was only nine years old when Chiksika invited him to come out on the next raid, all the other warriors were at least in their teens. Tecumapese was obviously concerned about sending a boy into battle but deferred to Chiksika's judgment. Tecumseh promised her that he would stay close to his older brother's side. That's easy to say for someone who has never experienced war, true bravery is more difficult to achieve. When the battle erupted, Tecumseh was overwhelmed with fear and ran away in panic. Hiding behind a log, he saw his brother get shot. Faced with such a dire circumstance, he overcame his fear and ran to help Chiksika, knowing he could easily be killed too. Their war party prevailed and his brother survived a near fatal gunshot wound. Even though he was brave enough to go back, Tecumseh felt shame and promised he would never succumb to fear again.

THINK: Have you ever succumbed to fear?

By then, Kentucky was established as a county in the state of Virginia and the British were supplying the Shawnees with arms and ammunition out of their fort in Detroit to fight the American rebels. The constant attacks had not driven out Boone and the settlers but the Shawnees had burned cabins, destroyed crops, forced the abandonment of various settlements, killed a number of men and created a real food shortage which would grow more serious later in the year. It was too late to start new crops but the people of Boonesborough found the prior year's corn had blossomed and grew to a respectable yield. The corn was a welcome rescue in the battle against starvation but Blackfish was winning the war.

In January of 1778 Boonesborough's salt supply was running low. Salt was very important for preserving food and adding flavor to an otherwise bland frontier diet. Boone took 28 men to Blue Licks, an especially good salt spring. It would typically take 840 gallons of weak brine to boil down into a bushel of salt, but a good spring could do it with 80 gallons. A bushel of salt was worth a cow and a half. It was warm work boiling the spring water until it all evaporated leaving only the salt. Winter was a good time to do it and the Indians generally stayed close to their towns in wintertime. The work crew would remain for a month when they would be relieved by another crew and the process would continue through the winter until a year's supply of salt was made. With his scouts in the area, Boone went out for a couple of nights to check his trap lines for meat and furs. A winter storm came upon him followed by a Shawnee war party. His knife was covered with frozen buffalo blood and he was unable to defend himself. Daniel Boone was captured by the Shawnees.

Brother Sheltowee

When he was brought back to the Shawnee's town across the river, he noticed more than 100 Indian chiefs dressed for war, led by Blackfish himself. He knew the British were encouraging a coordinated invasion and he could see that it was strong enough to destroy Boonesborough. The chiefs wanted vengeance for another senseless killing of a popular chief who was on a peace mission to a white fort; the British took advantage of the situation and stoked the Indians' anger. Among the chiefs gathered, Boone recognized the one who had taken him captive nine years earlier. "How d'do Captain Will?" he said as the two shook hands cordially. There was always a chivalrous tone to Daniel Boone's warfare with the Indians. He hated killing. He was never cruel (there is no evidence that he ever took a scalp), and he was never the victim of cruelty himself. The Indians admired and respected him. When someone's life is built on such a solid foundation, admiration and respect usually follow.

Boone convinced Blackfish to let the other salt makers surrender, and to wait until spring to take Boonesborough. By then the women and children would be more easily transportable to be sold as prisoners to the British if not adopted into the tribe. Most of the men were already in hand and could be used as slaves or more valuable war prisoners to sell to the British. Blackfish knew he would need the aid of the British for a major offensive which could not be undertaken until summer anyway. Boone also appealed to their religious convictions saying that killing them would displease the Great Spirit so they could not expect future success in hunting nor war. "Spare them" he said "and the Great Spirit will smile upon you." Blackfish agreed.[59]

Tecumseh was glad the salt makers were not going to face the torture and burning at the stake that filled him with such revulsion. However, the agreement said nothing about Boone who was forced to run the gauntlet. Everyone in town came out and formed two lines facing each other about eight feet apart. Men, women and children of all ages held clubs and sticks of varying thicknesses to strike the prisoner as he ran between them. If he made it to the end of the line at the council house, his ordeal would be over. Tecumseh and Tecumapese stood at the end of the line with small sticks, as neither of them liked the tradition. The end of the line was generally a poor position because prisoners often didn't make it that far. This was one of those times. Boone surprised the Indians by zig zagging from side to side to avoid the worst punishment and ultimately rammed his head into the chest of one brave who stepped into the middle. The Shawnees howled in laughter when the five foot seven inch solid rock Daniel Boone knocked their larger tribal brother out of the way. Boone survived the ordeal well and once it was over the tribe crowded around to congratulate him on his courage.

In March the prisoners were brought to Detroit to sell to the British, but Blackfish decided to keep Boone who was as good a woodsman as any of them and a better marksman. Such were valuable in any camp. He was adopted into the tribe as Chief Blackfish's son and given the name Sheltowee, meaning Big Turtle. By springtime, Rebecca Boone and the families of the other men went back to North Carolina thinking their husbands were all dead.

As spring came, Blackfish broke his forces into small war parties to go out along the frontier and wreak havoc. It was not uncommon for the Shawnees to adopt captives like Sheltowee and one war party came back that spring with two young girls after scalping the rest of their family. Margaret and Elizabeth McKinzie were adopted into Tecumseh's family as Little Sun and Little Moon and he promised to teach them to speak Shawnee if they would teach him English. Meanwhile, Boone was being treated as Blackfish's son and played games with the other Indians being careful not to beat them by too much.

They showed "the greatest expressions of joy when they exceeded me; and, when the reverse happened, of envy."[60] He showed them how he would load and fire his flintlock rifle on the run. It involved pouring the correct amount of gunpowder into the small muzzle hole from a powder horn, then dropping in a lead ball, freeing the ramrod from its holder and jamming it down the muzzle to pack the charge and returning the ramrod to its holder. Then finally, without spilling any, pouring another small amount of gunpowder into the pan to create the flash when struck by the flint that ignites the charge. All while running. There is no record of any Indian ever being able to do it, not even Tecumseh, although many tried. Boone also endeared himself to his new family with his sense of humor, playing jokes and enjoying when they were played on him. His pleasing nature and acceptance among the tribe proved the virtue of humility.

THINK: Are you friendly with adversaries?

Also proving that temperance is a virtue, he stashed away jerked venison meat and conserved his gunpowder and lead shot using only half measures when he hunted small game. One day he asked the chief if he could train his horse out in the cane field. It was the first time he asked for such latitude. Blackfish consented and also sent sentries to hide in the cane that commonly grew to 20 feet tall, to keep watch that he didn't escape. Boone knew he was being watched and came back to prove his loyalty. He wisely built his credibility with Chief Blackfish over the next few months.

As the weather got warm, the Shawnees' passion for battle was also heating up. Warriors were arriving from far away and Boone knew the attack on Boonesborough would be soon. On June 16, 1778 it was time to escape. After 4 months of captivity and 4 days escaping through the wilderness, Daniel Boone came back to a welcome fort but an empty home. Only Jemima was there with her new husband. His wife Rebecca and the rest of his family, for whom he brought a buffalo tongue, were gone. He did receive a warm welcome from his cat who remained. Tecumseh asked Blackfish if he thought they would ever see Sheltowee again. "I think we will see him again but only as an enemy. Not as a son or brother. We will see him when we attack Boonesborough, which will be very soon."

Under Siege

Knowing that Boone would have warned the inhabitants of Boonesborough, Blackfish postponed the attack until September 6th when four hundred Indians and twelve Canadians with British armaments assembled for the offensive. Ten year old Tecumseh was the youngest to go out on the expedition; the next in age was thirteen. The Shawnees, with less than expected help from the British, surrounded the fort at Boonesborough and offered its inhabitants favorable terms if they surrendered. Boone refused, saying they would fight until the last soul was alive.

After some negotiating, Blackfish said he did not know the settlers had purchased the land from the Cherokees, so he proposed a peace treaty where they would live as brothers with the Ohio River providing the boundary. It seemed too good to be true, and understanding the Shawnee language, Boone sensed a trick at the treaty signing and outwitted the Shawnees before they could grab him during a supposed ceremonial handshake. Boone and the other signers retreated to the fort, under a hail of bullets and arrows, where a siege lasted for eight more days. During the siege, the settlers noticed the clean river turned muddy when passing the fort. They deduced that the Shawnees were attempting to tunnel in but they had no way of knowing their route. After days of putting out fires caused by flaming arrows, a steady rain provided a respite from the fire and replenished declining water stocks inside the fort. The rain also revealed the Indians' tunnel which was washed away along with their hopes of taking the fort. The Shawnees retreated in exasperation hearing that reinforcements were coming to the aid of Boonesborough.

After the siege settled down, acrimony filled Boonesborough with Boone accused of treason and court marshaled for becoming so close to his Shawnee captors. It is unfathomable to believe that someone who sacrificed so much would be treated in such a way by the beneficiaries of his kindness. It was an entirely different kind of hardship for the man who faced so much. Maybe it reflects the hardship that all the settlers were facing that they would lash out in such a way. People under stress often act irrationally. Fortunately, the truth won out at trial when he was completely exonerated and promoted for the wisdom he displayed through his actions. Feeling estranged from his community, he went back east to get Rebecca and they would come back and build a new settlement nearby where he had a land claim.

> **THINK: Have you ever been unfairly accused?**

US forces were building up in the region and many of the tribes sought peace. George Washington was now the commanding general of the Continental Army of the American Revolution and laid out a plan to fight the British backed Indians by carrying "the war vigorously into their own country."[61] He was focused primarily on the Iroquois but the Shawnees figured they would be next. The five Shawnee tribes split between those who would continue to fight and those who sought peace. The latter group moved to the southwest.

Tecumseh's family remained and the war quieted down somewhat as Washington focused on the Iroquois. Tecumseh and the girls taught each other their respective languages and he was just about the only person who would show any kindness to his noisy brother. Lowawluwaysica had become even more obnoxious since discovering alcohol, and turned his older brother onto the rum they would often loot from captured forts. The misfit brother had lost an eye in a hunting accident which made him even more odious. Tecumseh and his brother had a common bond with alcohol which they both liked; it made Tecumseh mellow, humorous, and even silly. Like so many other adolescents, it seemed harmless to him, even beneficial. It will come to almost kill him.

Through much of the summer of 1779, Tecumseh would use his English skills and clothing taken from captives to lure white river travelers into ambushes by posing as a white boy needing help. He grew uncomfortable with the ambushes though, finding it distasteful to attack defenseless women and children rather than other warriors. At 11 years old, he was growing philosophical. Don't worry if you haven't felt philosophical yet, there is reason to believe that children's brains matured at an earlier age back then, but Tecumseh was exceptional by any standard.

A supply vessel had been ambushed with wonderful loot like armaments and food that delighted the tribe. All Tecumseh took was a jug of rum which he drank while the others were running the prisoners through the gauntlet before executing them. The rum numbed the pain he felt from hearing the prisoners shrieking in agony as they were burned at the stake.

Blackfish died from his mounting battle wounds and the other war chiefs sent strong demands to Detroit commanding the British, who begged them to take up the hatchet against the Americans, to provide troops and artillery to help with their assaults against the forts in Kentucky. The British agreed to a large invasion to take place in the spring after the wheat and melons had been planted. In the meantime they would continue to pay for scalps and prisoners.

Chiksika told Tecumseh that he was needed to catch food so he wanted him to remain back at camp the next winter and not out fighting. He killed so much game that his tribe remained fed, unlike others who were starving after their villages and crops were destroyed by US troops. Tecumseh played down his accomplishments at evening talk times, as if embarrassed by his heroics. His noisy brother showed no such modesty, bragging about the most insignificant achievements even as he shirked most responsibilities. Chiksika and Tecumapese had striven to instill in all the boys a deep and abiding love for the truth, in most cases successfully. Tecumseh was sad that his beloved sister, five years a widow, had become the wife of another brave and would be leaving. Although happy that his sister had again found love, losing her added to the sorrow that was building in his heart.

Redcoats Come Through

Four years into the Revolutionary War in June of 1780, more than 500 Indian warriors gathered with more than 100 British redcoats and 75 Canadian Rangers. Most important was a huge British cannon that could make a shambles of any Kentucky fort. After meeting up with additional warriors, the force numbered 1,250 men, the largest ever seen in the Kentucky territory. The army moved by river and planned to demolish and plunder a series of forts, including Boonesborough. Word spread and settlers were abandoning their cabins and taking refuge inside nearby forts.

The force came upon its first target using their huge cannon to blow a hole in the side of Ruddell's Station. The commander promptly surrendered his fort but his people were not granted the safe passage they were promised.

Instead a melee ensued with Indians killing and scalping men, women and children. Chiksika had one boy by the arm but Tecumseh said "I'll take him Chiksika." In his best English he urgently told the boy "Don't fight, you will be killed if you do." The rest of his family was killed and Tecumseh brought the boy, Stephen Ruddell, out of the chaos as the British Captain halted the fighting in disgust at what he saw. "Chiefs!" he shouted, "What kind of warriors are these that act in this way against people who have laid down their arms and surrendered in good faith."[62] The captain made every chief promise not to repeat the massacre again or he was going to take his troops and cannon back to Detroit. They agreed, and the next fort surrendered without a shot being fired. Loaded with prisoners and plunder, the captain said they had made their point and were turning back. The Americans would surely leave the area now that they have seen the force of British arms.

The Indians were incensed, they had finally gotten the weapons they needed but were now being deprived of what the British had promised them. The short lived invasion of Kentucky was over and the Shawnees were carrying as much plunder as they could and more prisoners than they had ever handled. They should have been overjoyed but anger and despair prevailed instead. Tecumseh asked Chiksika what happens next. Chiksika said "We have become the bee that stung the bear."[63] It wouldn't be long until the bear tried to squash the bee.

When they got back to Ohio, Stephen Ruddell was made to run the gauntlet and did so well that they adopted him into Tecumseh's family. He enjoyed learning the Shawnee ways as he and Tecumseh tried to only converse in the other's language. Adolescence is a great time to learn another language due to the unique state of the teenage brain. Take advantage of the opportunity to build those neural circuits before the pathways are converted to highways. Meanwhile, the McKinzie girls were teaching Tecumseh table manners and how to hold and use eating utensils. The girls had learned well and taken over the wigwam duties in the absence of Tecumapese. Chiksika thought it would take a while for the Americans to put together a strong enough response, so he took Tecumseh on a trip to the tribes in the Southwest.

Daniel Boone had established his new home at Boone's Station a few miles north of Boonesborough. Hearing that land grants were being issued in Virginia, he collected almost $50,000 in investments and went to make a claim. On his way he checked into an inn and was robbed while he slept. He said he must have been drugged by the innkeeper. Otherwise it is hard to imagine that a woodsman who would wake at the slightest noise slept while his room was being ransacked.[64] It was another financial disaster for Daniel Boone but his investors remained confident in the man who built his life on such a solid foundation. Exemplifying George Washington's 44th rule, they did not blame him because they never doubted his integrity.

Disaster also came to the Shawnees as the bear struck back. Chiksika and Tecumseh were saddened on their return to see most of the Shawnee towns had been burned down by a force of more than 1,000 US troops. Tecumseh asked Chiksika how Moneto could let this happen to the Shawnees, a people who took such good care of nature. He was having his first crisis of faith. Tecumseh knew that Moneto punished behavior he disapproves of, but he was so blinded by his anger towards the whites that he couldn't see any errors in the Shawnee ways. Deep inside, he knew, because it ate at him every time he heard prisoners scream.

THINK: Do you ever wonder why God lets bad things happen?

The Warrior Goes to Town

After Tecumseh's twelfth summer, he was honored with full tribal warrior status, the youngest in the Shawnee history that was meticulously recorded. That was also the age at which Daniel Boone got his first gun. Both young men were given greater responsibilities than their peers as they spent their youth preparing their lives for greatness, maybe not consciously but through diligently developing their skills and talents. As a warrior, Tecumseh was now able to lead war parties on his own. In his shoulder length glossy black hair he could wear the emblem of his rank, a single or double white-tipped eagle feather affixed to a brass medallion and attached just over his ear, with the tips trailing downward over his shoulder. It was a symbol of rank that allowed him to attend and vote at any council meetings. His rank also allowed him to travel to the cosmopolitan capital city of the Miami Indians to the north, Kekionga, at a crossroads of rivers leading to and from the Great Lakes. Tecumseh had never seen such a real city with permanent buildings and several trading posts selling a wider range of products than he had ever imagined even existed.

The Miami chief lived in a spacious log cabin with glass window panes and upholstered furniture. It was a coming of age for Tecumseh to meet the great chief, especially when he was complimented on becoming a warrior at such a young age. The chief told him "You have the eyes of your father, I see courage and determination behind them."[65] Tecumseh was taken aback by the compliment before the chief abruptly departed. He had received plenty of compliments throughout his life but being recognized by such an esteemed person was a distinct honor. The Shawnees went out to enjoy their visit to Kekionga, a city frequented by British and Canadian soldiers and European traders mingling with Indians from various tribes. The buzz around town was that their father across the ocean, King George, was getting ready to make peace in Paris with the Americans. Chiksika said he would keep his promise to Pucksinwah and never make peace with the white man, Tecumseh said "Nor I."[66]

Peace was far from the frontier in October of 1780 when Daniel Boone and his brother Edward went out to make salt. Indians came upon them and Edward was killed and decapitated as Daniel hid in the cane field. The Indians thought they got the legend himself but it was just another tragedy to afflict the Boone family. Like all the other adversity, it only made him stronger. By this time, Daniel had been appointed county sheriff and held other titles of political prominence. He was captured by British troops at one point and either escaped or was paroled, there is dispute as to which. It is indisputable that wherever he went, Daniel Boone commanded respect. Probably because he treated others with respect, even his adversaries.

The Shawnees continued their raids with an especially severe one on a pair of riverboats. After killing dozens of settlers aboard, only a handful of women and children remained clustered in a terrified huddle. The dead around them were being scalped and mutilated and it got worse. The babies were ripped from their mothers' arms and tomahawked and scalped. A sole survivor was brutally mutilated and left impaled on a stake as a warning to others coming down the river. The Shawnees were cackling in their amusement but Tecumseh was disgusted by the brutality. He swore to never again stand by silently in the face of such atrocities.

It took a few years until he got the chance. When he was 15, his war party came upon a group of campers in a hidden ravine. The Shawnees surprised the whites, attacking them with clubs and tomahawks. Tecumseh moved with unmatched skill and poise, killing four campers while always knowing exactly where his tribal brothers were in the commotion of the fight. The sole survivor was brought back to the Shawnee's camp to be burned at the stake. With his arms tied behind his back a circle of fire was lit around the victim and the coals were gradually moved closer until he slowly singed and burned to a crisp as the tribe cheered and jeered. Tecumseh was revolted by the senseless brutality and stopped an elder chief from poking the charred remains. He declared to his elder and the rest of the warriors "there is no honor in the torturing of any man."[67] After much arguing about Shawnee tradition, Tecumseh said "If the choice lies between tradition and honor, who here would choose tradition? I do not and cannot believe Moneto could approve of such cowardice, of such desire to inflict unnecessary pain." He agreed that the man deserved death for coming into their territory but not the death of a rat. "How have we the right to call ourselves warriors, or even men, if we act in such manner?" Then he said "Never will I consider a friend any man who will allow himself to take part in so degrading a measure."[68]

The tribe was stunned. Chiksika eventually seconded Tecumseh's point, saying his younger brother is wiser and a better fighter than any of them and predicting he will one day be a great Shawnee chief. Then a couple of others added their consent and more followed. Finally, the oldest chief in attendance rose and said of Tecumseh "Shawnees everywhere will learn of his bravery this day, and of his wisdom. I gladly make the same vow."[69] At 15 years old, Tecumseh convinced his tribe to abandon their repulsive tradition. He had become a Shawnee superstar. It may have gone to his head a little bit.

Their towns and farmland having been burned by US troops, Tecumseh's war party went south to warmer climates for the winter. On the way, they came upon a herd of buffalo. As the others took aim with guns and arrows, Tecumseh, who had been drinking rum from his flask all day, galloped off on his horse into the rushing herd. Catching up to one bull, he put his knife in his teeth and jumped onto the animal in mid sprint. Struggling to hold on, he took his knife and went to cut the buffalo's jugular vein but he missed. The bull jumped and Tecumseh went flying off into the stampeding herd. He was kicked and pummeled as the herd of wild beasts, each weighing up to a ton, passed over him. The others rode quickly to the rescue shooting their guns to scare the herd away. They took Tecumseh's mangled body to their camp and nurtured him back to consciousness. His hip was broken and the bone almost came through the skin. He would take a while to heal so they had to remain in place for some time. Chiksika scolded him saying that he was very lucky to be alive after such a stupid stunt. Tecumseh nodded and winced at the pain a slight motion caused. "It was the liquor, wasn't it?" He said. Chiksika said "Yes. It is bad. It robs us of good sense. It makes us do things that we are otherwise too smart to do, things dangerous to ourselves and others." "From this time forward," Tecumseh vowed in his pain, "no liquid except water will ever again pass my lips."[70] Having suffered through such a painful lesson, he never broke that vow.

> **THINK: Have you learned any painful lessons?**

Seeking Peace

That was the autumn of 1783 when the Treaty of Paris ended the Revolutionary War. Someone told King George that he heard Washington was going to retire after the war. The King could not imagine giving up so much power as Washington had earned. He famously said "If he does that he will be the greatest man in the world." Washington did exactly that and earned even more respect from his countrymen who elected him as their first president a few years later. It was an office which he again could have held for life but that would have been counter to the whole purpose of the Revolution, so he retired after two terms in office. It is difficult to appreciate how revolutionary Washington's retirement was. Up to that point in world history, leaders had not relinquished power voluntarily, it usually only happened at death, naturally or not. Tecumseh grew to be like Washington in that he always put his nation and his people before himself. In his later years, he saw how effective Washington was at uniting the disparate American states and he wanted to do the same with the various Indian tribes. He reverted to his nomadic Shawnee roots and travelled among other tribes helping to fight their wars against the encroaching white settlers. His political power grew enormously, but like

Washington, that wasn't his motivator. He simply followed his conscience and did what he thought was right.

Daniel Boone had brought his family back to Kentucky and more disaster struck when his son Israel was killed at the Battle of Blue Licks. At age 15, it was one of Tecumseh's first major battles although it is not known if the scalp he bagged was Israel Boone's. Daniel had to leave his slain son behind as he escaped the battle where the Shawnees and British Loyalists routed the Americans. Of all the horrors of his long life, this episode made the deepest impression on him. Thirty years later he could not describe it without tears. Boone wrote to the governor of Virginia saying Kentucky had to be either reinforced or abandoned. The reinforcements would gradually come. After the Treaty of Paris ended the Revolutionary War, the raids slowed down but they didn't end. Even President George Washington had to cancel a planned trip to the area years later out of fear of Indian attacks.

The battle of Blue Licks practically closed out the Revolutionary War and opened a relatively peaceful time in Daniel Boone's troubled life. By 1786, Boone had become an innkeeper hired by the US government to feed and care for Indian prisoners. By most accounts he treated them like guests at his inn. With the war of the Kentucky frontier being largely won, a prisoner exchange was arranged. Tecumseh, Chiksika and other Shawnee warriors came together with Boone, Kenton and other settlers and exchanged dozens of prisoners, some who had been adopted into their new families on either side and did not want to return. Tecumseh's nephew was one who couldn't stop raving about the comfortable life he lived and the school he attended. It sickened Tecumseh to see him pledge never to take up arms against his white father. Likewise, some whites wanted to remain with their new Shawnee families, Steven Ruddell was one. After the exchange, Indians and settlers joined in a cookout with food that each side brought, followed by singing and dancing. Among the good relations however, there remained an undercurrent of animosity. When a settler recognized his dead friend's horse, a fight broke out but Boone and Kenton intervened to keep the peace and bought the horse from the Shawnees. As they all went their separate ways, some of the settlers stole some Indian horses leaving an otherwise constructive evening on a sour note. Achieving peace proved to be a distant goal even though everyone was weary from years of war.

Although he didn't smoke, Boone grew tobacco since it was such a good cash crop. Near his cabin, he erected a three tiered curing shed for his product. One day in 1795, a group of his old Shawnee captors came upon him. From the upper tier where he was laying the tobacco, he stalled for time with friendly small talk as he gathered a pile of the large pungent leaves. The friendly banter disguised their troubled history and at the right time, he threw the pile of tobacco down on top of the Indians, smothering them as he ran away. Making it to his cabin, he looked back to see the Shawnees still struggling beneath the large pile of stinky leaves, cursing him and themselves for letting the master fool them again.

Boone eventually went to Missouri and again became the leading man in his community. As magistrate of the Spanish crown, who ruled that inland part of the American continent, he dealt justice. Holding court under the "Justice Tree" near his cabin, he heard cases and awarded penalties according to methods of his own devising. It was rough and tumble justice but it was what his community wanted. There were no complaints. One day he ran into a group of Shawnees out hunting. The group included one of his adoptive sisters, Blackfish's daughter, and one of his salt makers who returned to living with the tribe after a brief return to white civilization. There was no battle this time just friendly reminiscing.

The Prophet

Tecumseh's stature and reputation grew and tribes far and wide were clamoring for the tall slender warrior to lead their war parties against the whites. Chiksika was killed in battle in 1789 after predicting Tecumseh would be the greatest and most powerful leader the Indians have ever known, praising his brother for building an unprecedented brotherhood of Indians.[71] Tecumseh was now hard at work on his objective to build a united Indian nation like George Washington was doing with the Seventeen Fires, as he called the states (his native Ohio was the 17th.)

Lowawluwaysica became Tenskwatawa, meaning The Prophet as part of a political scheme with Tecumseh. The obnoxious brother noticed another tribe's prophet had the power to condemn people to death for baseless offenses like witchcraft. He thought it could be an effective way to build political power within the amalgamation of tribes that Tecumseh was building. This demonstrates the difference with Washington, who rallied his troops with eloquence and example and did not use trickery like The Prophet, who condemned his opposition to death for practicing witchcraft. With remarkable alacrity, The Prophet assumed greater responsibilities for his tribe's culture and decisions. He convinced them to shun the ways of the whites, including drinking and smoking. Like other religious leaders through the ages, it was a matter of "do as I say, and not as I do" as The Prophet continued to enjoy his rum. Intermarriage was especially offensive as he and Tecumseh were promoting a philosophy of an Indian master race. This was a century before Nietzsche thought of it.

Unlike Tecumseh, his phony brother was all about himself, building his own power. When Tecumseh would travel, The Prophet would predict things like comets and eclipses that Tecumseh told him would occur. Some think Tecumseh learned about comets and eclipses from the books he stole from river ambushes while others believe he was actually able to predict the future. He predicted the massive New Madrid earthquake of December 16, 1811, which could not have been in any book. In the preceding months, Tecumseh travelled to many tribes in an effort to unite them in a war against the encroaching whites. He consulted with the Choctaws, Chickasaws, Cherokees, and Santees in the Southeast, then further south along the gulf coast with the Biloxis, Creeks, Alabamas and Seminoles, then back north and west to visit The Calusa, Yazoos, Natchez, Tawakomias and the Caddos. Maybe he saw that Thirteen Fires worked well as a start for Washington. He presented each tribe with a bundle of sticks to be burned at each of the next full moons. Before the fifth moon, a great sign would signal that the nation will be born in 30 days, so the last stick should be cut into 30 pieces and one burned each night.

When he got to the southern tribes, his message was not well received. They lived mostly in peace alongside the whites and Tecumseh failed to see the wisdom in that arrangement. They were already most of the way where Tecumseh wanted to go. The southern chiefs were hostile to Tecumseh and his thirst for war. Tecumseh told them if they did not join his confederation he would "stamp my foot to the ground and awaken our great mother earth...She will cause your houses to fall to the ground and the bones of every man to tremble with the trembling of the ground...and great trees will lean and fall though there be no wind...And when she thus reveals to you her inner heart, then you must...rise with one mind and one heart against those whites who have so defiled her."[72]

Sure enough, before the fifth moon, a great meteor appeared that was seen from the Rocky Mountains to the east coast and as far north as Canada and south to Florida. Another Great Panther Passing Across was surely the intended sign. Indians across the continent began to break their final sticks into 30 pieces. 30 days after the meteor, Tecumseh found himself where the Ohio River meets the Mississippi, in New Madrid, Missouri, looking for his sister. While camping on the night of December 16, 1811, the land beneath the Shawnees' camp liquefied, and trees and everything else all around fell. Tecumseh's prediction had come true. Their camp was within a few miles of the epicenter of the largest earthquake ever to strike the eastern part of North America. It was felt for 1,000 miles in every direction waking President James Madison and churning up waters on the Gulf coast as well as the Great Lakes, it even made the Mississippi River flow backwards for a while. The massive earthquake convinced Indians across the land that Tecumseh did indeed make the earth move and that his nation was about to be born.

So however the info came to being, The Prophet had some good material to work with. The fact that his predictions came true was the only reason why anyone would listen to such a despicable person. However, it was the Shawnee's prophet back in 1771 who truly had a premonition. The third child of Pucksinwah's triplets did indeed bring disaster upon his people. While Tecumseh was traveling in search for his sister, The Prophet took the bait of the American general and future president, William Henry Harrison, in the Battle of Tippecanoe. He ignored his brother's explicit instructions and led the Shawnees into a terrible military defeat. The debacle destroyed a decade's worth of Tecumseh's work building a united Indian nation like George Washington did with the Seventeen Fires. Tecumseh explicitly warned his brother not to be provoked because he had a premonition that it was going to happen; including that he would perish on a battlefield in the same War of 1812.

The war was still raging on October 4, 1813, the night before his final battle, when Tecumseh distributed each of his weapons among his favorite warrior brothers. He saved the war club that Chiksika gave him as his only weapon for the next day's fight. His war party was teaming with a British regiment preparing for battle against General Harrison east of Detroit in today's Ontario, Canada. They selected a patch of dry ground in a marshy area where McGregor's Creek flows into the Thames River. Tecumseh warned his brother braves about his premonition instructing them to immediately retreat if he went down in battle as it would foretell a wider Indian defeat. Legend says Tecumseh painted his face black that day. On the field of battle at the site now marked as Tecumseh Park, it was his dear friend of 25 years, Chaubenee, who saw him take two bullets in his lower left chest and fall down dead. He instantly threw his head back and shrieked "Tecumseh is dead! Retreat! Retreat!"[73]

> **THINK: How do you think the Shawnees felt at this seminal loss?**

Daniel Boone volunteered as a soldier in the War of 1812 but they wouldn't take him. He was too old at 78. He made his last trip to Kentucky in 1817 and paid off all his debts saying "I can now die in peace." Like the survivalist he always was, he lived a few more years and died in 1820 at age 85 with a half a dollar to his name. Boone, Tecumseh, and George Washington were all great men but like everyone, they all had their flaws. After losing their fathers in their early adolescent years, all three lived mostly virtuous lives and fully developed their intellects and personal talents. None of them were religious by most definitions of the word, but the seven holy virtues were integral to the personalities of all three. They were all incredibly giving of themselves and were recognized as great for being so selfless. Each of them spent their youth building a solid rock foundation upon which they built their great lives.

George Washington died in 1799, two years after leaving office, in comfortable wealth. More importantly, with the iconic stature as the only leader of a revolution who ever defeated a colonial power in the history of the world. Daniel Boone died at peace with the love of his family and the respect and admiration of his nation, including his enemies. Tecumseh also died with the love of his family and the respect and admiration of his nation and his foes; but as his biographer Allan Eckert titled his book, he died with a sorrow in his heart.

For all of his greatness, Tecumseh's anger towards the whites dominated his life and prevented him from fulfilling his dreams. A man who knew himself so well, who overcame what he probably thought was his greatest weakness, alcohol, failed to recognize how his anger was keeping him from reaching his potential. If he had been willing to make peace as so many other tribes did, he may have been able to build that Indian nation as a neighbor to the United States. As bad as it was to see his dreams of an Indian nation go unfulfilled, it may have been more painful to see his beloved Tecumapese reject the Indian life to move in with a French trader who lived in a cabin.

Chapter 6: ...and Roll

To be, or not to be - that is the question:
Whether 'tis nobler in the mind to suffer
The slings and arrows of outrageous fortune
Or to take arms against a sea of troubles,
And by opposing end them.

- Hamlet

Those are the most famous words in all of literature. Written around 1600 by William Shakespeare, the title character of *The Tragedy of Hamlet, Prince of Denmark* does quite a bit of talking, so much so that playing him on stage is a feather in any actor's cap. Hamlet is known for his soliloquies which are long speeches while alone on stage. In the most famous one above he is contemplating suicide, his way of opposing and ending all of his troubles including unbearable grief from the murder of his father, King Hamlet of Denmark, by his uncle Claudius who quickly assumed the throne and married his sister-in-law, Hamlet's mother Queen Gertrude. If that's not bad enough, his father's ghost has told Hamlet that he will be trapped in purgatory until Hamlet avenges his death. That's a lot to ask of a grieving young prince.

After debating with himself for about twenty lines, he realizes *"Thus conscience does make cowards of us all"* and decides not to take the action that any audience at the time would have seen as among the most grievous of sins. We see later in the play that suicide prohibited people of those times from even being buried in a cemetery. Audiences before modern times would not have recognized mental illness and would see it as an unambiguous truth. Shakespeare pairs this concept with incest as clearly being wrong. Both are themes sprinkled throughout the four hour fictional play that juxtaposes such basic truths against moral ambiguities that confront all of our lives. Hamlet struggles with uncertainty and passes up an opportunity to do the deed that is called of him. As the play's title suggests, the consequences are tragic.

The Uncertainty of Truth

Hamlet uses his considerable intellect, honed by his studies at the university in Wittenberg, to confront common questions of life. He deals extensively with the only certain truth in all lives, death. The views on suicide echo the views of the Catholic Church which was the arbiter of truth up to that time. Wittenberg is where Martin Luther challenged the Catholic Church in 1517 setting off the Great Schism of Christianity and the birth of Protestantism. It is unknown if Shakespeare joined his family in illegally practicing Catholicism after King Henry VIII established the Church of England in 1534. Having a ghost as a main character, especially his father's state in purgatory, is an acknowledgment of the Catholic Church's expressed truth of the afterlife. On the other hand, the admonition to take vengeance is in opposition to Church teaching that vengeance belongs to God alone. It is but one contradiction in a play welling with them. Hamlet struggles with his dilemma as he even struggles with the appearance of the ghost. His father had come to him previously in his *"mind's eye"* or a dream, but this time was in the presence of others, so it is an established fact. Although he witnessed the ghost, Hamlet's close friend Horatio did not hear the ghost explain his murder by his brother who poured poison in his ear while napping in his garden. The ghost demands Hamlet, his friend Horatio, and a guard named Marcellus to swear their secrecy about seeing him. Marcellus famously says *"Something is rotten in the state of Denmark."*

This is our first look at the close friendship between Hamlet and Horatio, we will see other friends but none who Hamlet can confide in like he does with Horatio. He not only trusts Horatio but clearly enjoys his company. They discuss philosophical concepts and explore the meaning of life together. Aristotle is 2,500 years old to us while he was almost 2,000 years old to Shakespeare, and just as classic and relevant then as now. Shakespeare was certainly well versed in the Nicomachean Ethics and portrays the friendship between Hamlet and Horatio as one that reached Aristotle's highest level.

Hamlet and Horatio have shared a surreal experience together and are not quite sure what to make of it. It certainly can't be explained by anything they learned in school. Speaking philosophically, Hamlet casts a skeptical eye towards the views that emanated from Wittenberg telling his close friend from the university *"There are more things in heaven and earth, Horatio, Than are dreamt of in your philosophy."* This is a counterintuitive assertion that religious theology is deeper and more complex than Enlightenment philosophy, and another nod towards the Catholic Church. Horatio thought Hamlet was acting mad but Hamlet told him to prepare to see even stranger behavior in the future. This brings up more uncertainty as the audience cannot be sure if Hamlet has in fact gone mad. Shakespeare uses the confusion as a literary tool to symbolize how truth is often hidden by uncertainty.

> **THINK: Have you ever had trouble discerning the truth in a situation?**

Hamlet is an enigma to the audience as he has been to thinkers in the four hundred years since Shakespeare created the character. Depending on how a given actor and director choose to present the text, the play provides latitude for different perspectives. That's one of the interesting aspects of the live theater art form, the playwright creates the characters through the words they speak and the actions they take, but the directors and actors add their own interpretation to the work of art by the tones of voice they use and the movements they make. Some productions have been based on Sigmund Freud's interpretation of Hamlet as an example of the Oedipus complex where sons desire their mothers in a sexual way. Freud saw most of life in a sexual way. The play's frequent allusions to incest lend credence to that interpretation while its shocking nature accentuates the fact that certain truths are unassailable. Audiences of any era certainly see the clarity that incest is wrong. Some directors even choose to portray the love between Ophelia and her brother Laertes as more than Platonic. The characters are the grown children of Polonius, Claudius' counselor who was politically adept enough to remain in that position after similarly serving King Hamlet. We surmise that from the families' close relationship.

Polonius is a symbol of Shakespeare's disdain for the politics of his day. He is able to serve both kings because he is a simple "yes man" telling his boss whatever he wants to hear. We see an exposition on his sincerity when he bids farewell with fatherly advice to Laertes who is leaving to study in France. As Wittenberg is symbolic of Protestantism, France was the dominant Catholic world power at the end of the 16th century, having survived a hundred years of religious civil wars. It was the world's superpower at that time. The dichotomy between Wittenberg and France highlights the contrast between the wavering Hamlet and the resolute Laertes that we see as the story plays out. Polonius gives his departing son mostly trite advice about not having too much fun and showing discretion in one's behavior but he finishes with another unambiguous truth: *"This above all - to thine own self be true, and it must follow, as the night the day, Thou canst not then be false to any man."* He is saying that being true to yourself will keep you honest with others. Then showing the hypocrisy of a politician, he subsequently sends spies out to keep an eye on his son and report back about any vices that he might enjoy.

Despite the cynical perspective, Shakespeare reveals something that Hamlet woefully lacks. That is a mentor. Laertes has his father Polonius to guide him through the dramatic changes facing any adolescent. In this case the son is going away to school in a distant land. Hamlet doesn't have his father to play that role and to his further distress, he can't turn to his uncle who murdered his father. Maybe that's why he is so indecisive and confused. We all need people ahead of us on the path of life who can guide us along. So if you don't have one, try to find a mentor. When I was in high school, my employer played that role for me, he taught me things my father didn't. Things like dirty jokes or stereotypes or perspectives from his life that my father couldn't even imagine. My boss had survived the Nazi concentration camp at Buchenwald Germany. He never spoke about it but did show me the serial number tattooed on his arm. Being a holocaust survivor gave him unimpeachable moral authority to me. He told me about life's seedier side while demonstrating the empathy and decency that comes from adversity. One who has felt pain is not likely to inflict it on others. He learned life's lessons the hard way and I saw him as nothing but great. That made it so much more fun to learn about life's seedier side, which makes the good and true shine brighter. I never asked George to be my mentor, I just earned his respect by working hard and was receptive to his advice and stories. It's an example of good attracting good. As I progressed through subsequent stages of life, I had other mentors whose lessons were invaluable in helping me through the uncertainty and challenges that have been part of my life. Friends will come to you naturally but mentors must be sought out. Besides an employer, aunts, uncles, and grandparents are natural candidates to be mentors to you. Maybe there is a teacher who cares enough to take the extra time to help you find truth through all of life's confusion. As Shakespeare shows us, it isn't always clear.

THINK: Who could be a mentor to you?

Not surprisingly, King Claudius is another political leader portrayed in a negative light. Early in the play, news arrives that

Prince Fortinbras of Norway is leading an army into Denmark, presumably to take the kingdom in vengeance for the death of his father who perished at the hands of the deceased King Hamlet. However, Claudius receives word that the army merely wants to travel through Denmark on its way to fight in Poland. Hearing what he wants to hear, Claudius accepts it at face value and goes on with the celebration of his new monarchy. His nonchalance in dismissing the threat is striking. The selfish king only has time for his own pleasure. We see how there is something rotten indeed in the state of Denmark.

In the coming years you will be asked to believe all sorts of things from all sorts of people. Only you will be able to decide what you believe. Will you be like Claudius and only believe what you want to believe or will you sift through life's distractions and accept hard truths? By knowing yourself, and *to thine own self being true*, you will be able to separate truth from all the noise that constantly confronts us. Living the seven virtues will bring truth into clearer focus. Patience and diligence will reveal it; charity, humility and kindness will bring it upon you; chastity and temperance will keep the distractions from truth out of your way. These are the virtues that are so foreign to Claudius. Remember how Socrates saw virtue, knowledge and truth interchangeably. He saw truth as that which is good. It is when we get away from truth that our lives get away from being good. Hamlet can't accept the truth he sees in front of him and his life is dark and troubled. We see that is not only because he is without the guidance of a mentor, he is also confused about the girl he loves.

Method in Madness

Laertes and Polonius both tell Ophelia to forget about her love for Hamlet since a prince's marriage is determined by political considerations. Gertrude corrects that mistruth later in the play proclaiming she had always hoped that Hamlet would marry Ophelia. Her hopes are dashed by Ophelia's death which we assume was by suicide but again, we can't be sure. Shakespeare persistently portrays the uncertainty of life. Her drowning could have been accidental but it occurred after she had gone mad seeing Hamlet having gone mad.

Hamlet feigns madness to mask the grief he feels from plotting to kill his stepfather. He tells Horatio that he might see fit *"To put an antic disposition on."* Even though he said it is only a put on, his seeming madness makes the audience unsure if it has developed into true insanity. Polonius thinks Hamlet's unrequited love for his daughter has driven the prince insane and feels obliged to inform Claudius. *"Since brevity is the soul of wit,"* the counsel tells his king *"Your noble son is mad."* Claudius takes the advice and tells Gertrude that Ophelia is *"The head and source of all your son's distemper."* Notice how he absolves himself of any problem since Hamlet is her son, not his. This contrasts to earlier scenes when he claims to have no less love for Hamlet than a *"dearest father bears his son."* He spoke kindly earlier but now reveals his true self who can't be bothered by someone else's troubles. Unfortunately, you will come across many people like this in the years ahead, just remember Confucius and emulate the good and avoid the bad. Displaying the wisdom of a mother, Gertrude disagrees and attributes Hamlet's grief to *"his father's death and our o'erhasty marriage."* Polonius feels he is at fault for telling his daughter to stay away from the prince, he is sure that has made Hamlet crazy. To figure the truth out for themselves, they devise a scheme to spy on Hamlet and Ophelia when they are alone together. Before it is to happen, Polonius encounters Hamlet who is speaking strangely. Polonius listens and realizes *"Though this be madness, yet there is a method in't."* Aside to the audience he says *"How pregnant sometimes his replies are!"* The audience cannot be sure how much is method and how much is madness. More uncertainty.

Hamlet's plans are constantly being diverted by his thoughts on whether or not he really saw and heard what his fathers' ghost said. He could simply ask his close friend Horatio who also witnessed King Hamlet's ghost, but he is choosing not to see the uncomfortable truth. He contemplates that the devil himself could have taken his father's form, telling him to kill Claudius in order to damn his soul forever. Shakespeare is either giving a lesson on Catholic catechism or he is showing us the lengths to which Hamlet will go to avoid fulfilling his troublesome task. He fully explores his intellect to consider all the possibilities and decides that there are things *"more relative than this"* meaning there is a way to prove if the ghost's story is true. He concocts a plan to have a group of actors stage a play reenacting the murder. If it was true, Claudius would certainly react when seeing it. *"The play's the thing wherein I'll catch the conscience of the King."*

The Mousetrap

The play within a play is a dramatic device that Shakespeare uses in several of his plays. For this one, Hamlet asks a group of traveling actors if they could act out *"AEneas' tale to Dido"* referring to a scene from Virgil's Latin classic. Hamlet skillfully acts it out himself exhibiting his royal education as well as his sanity that the audience is beginning to question. He asks the actors to perform another story that with minor edits, replicates the story of the king's murder.

Earlier in the scene, Claudius and Gertrude had summoned Hamlet's childhood friends, Rosencrantz and Guildenstern, asking them to go speak with Hamlet and try to find out what is troubling him. Happy to see them, Hamlet asks how they are doing. Not great, but not bad, they tell him. The three old friends get in a philosophical conversation. Hamlet tells them *"for there is nothing either good or bad but thinking makes it so."* This would be called moral relativism today, where anyone can justify any thought or action claiming there is no such thing as absolute truth. The concept will create confusion in your life but if you believe that there is truth, living an ethical life will give you the self-confidence to see through the fog and identify the truth. Hamlet saw through the fog and discerned a truth in the visit of his old friends. When he asks them what brings them to the royal palace, Rosencrantz says *"To visit you, my lord; no other occasion.* " Hamlet thanks his friend but adds *"Were you not sent for?"* Guildenstern says *"What should we say, my lord?"* Hamlet says *"You were sent for; and there is a kind of confession in your looks, which your modesties have not craft enough to colour."* Hamlet's friends would be lousy poker players.

Take it as a warning that deception often shows through one's facial expressions. You will notice when someone's mannerisms betray a guilty conscience, something will seem wrong. Of course, that requires looking up from your screens and seeing your friends face to face. It is only by knowing your friends in such a personal way that you can discern what level of Aristotle's hierarchy they maintain. Hamlet tells his friends that their friendship requires them to be honest with him, so they admit that they were sent. With some trust established between them, Hamlet tells how unhappy he has been without divulging what is making him so unhappy. He gets philosophic saying *"What a piece of work is man...in action how like an angel! In apprehension how like a god!"* He considers his indecisiveness and dithering as godlike reason. He won't show such divine deliberation later in the play. He asks of mankind *"what is this quintessence of dust?"* echoing philosophers through the ages asking why we exist, as well as Catholic teaching that we all come from dust and to dust we will return. Seeing how depressed he is, Hamlet's friends do what friends should do and try to cheer him up. They tell him about his old favorite group of actors that are coming from the city. That does excite him and spawns the scheme to put on the play.

> **THINK: Are you adept at deception?**

Rosencrantz and Guildenstern report back to Claudius and Gertrude that they can't tell exactly what is bothering Hamlet but he seemed to be happy to hear his old favorite actors were coming to perform. Claudius and Gertrude are happy that Hamlet is happy and look forward to the play. When his one true friend enters,

Hamlet tells Horatio about his plan and asks him to watch the king for any reaction. Horatio gladly agrees and we hear trumpets and drums announcing the arrival of the royal couple. Hamlet cheerfully welcomes everyone and playfully sits with Ophelia. They look to be a happy couple. The others think he has overcome his troubles so everyone is festive. Part way through the performance, after the player queen expresses her love for her husband, Hamlet asks his mother what she thinks of the story. Gertrude responds with the famous line *"The lady doth protest too much, methinks."* She thinks the player queen's emphatic claims of love betray a guilty conscience. When someone protests too loudly that they did not do something, there's a good chance they did. Shakespeare is giving us another example of people failing at deception. The king asks Hamlet what the play is called and Hamlet says *"The Mousetrap."* It continues to when the player king is poisoned through his ear while napping. Knowing it must refer to him, Claudius immediately stands up, demands light, and storms out. Everyone else leaves too, except Hamlet and Horatio. The plan worked, Prince Hamlet now is certain of the truth that Claudius murdered King Hamlet. Claudius' reaction proved his guilt. There is nothing else to think about, or so we think. Rosencrantz and Guildenstern return to tell Hamlet that the king is very upset and the queen wants to speak with him in her room before he goes to bed.

The Mad Prince

King Claudius has a problem on his hands but nobody else except Hamlet and Horatio know the real meaning of the play. Claudius directs Rosencrantz and Guildenstern to bring Hamlet to England because it is unsafe to the monarchy to have an insane prince running around. The friends express their allegiance to their king, and not their childhood friend. They do not know that the king is also sending sealed orders with them that Hamlet is to be executed. While alone, Claudius ponders his predicament. He is feeling guilty and wants heavenly forgiveness but he realizes that would require first giving up what he has gained. Kneeling, he asks *"My crown, mine own ambition, and my queen. May one be pardon'd and retain th' offence?"* He isn't the Prodigal Son asking for forgiveness and willing to live like a servant. His greed for power and privilege is greater than his desire for salvation.

Hamlet comes up behind him. Here is his opportunity. He is certain of his uncle's guilt and therefore the veracity of his father's ghost. *"Now might I do it pat"* whispers the prince. But Hamlet sees Claudius in prayer, a state of grace. Remember, Christian theology says it is never too late to gain salvation by repenting and asking for forgiveness. His father's ghost explained how he was cut from life before having a chance to confess his own sins, and gain such a state of grace for himself. That is why he now suffers *"confin'd to fast in fires"* of purgatory. Killing Claudius now would send him straight to heaven, *"Why, this is hire and salary, not revenge!"* Hamlet again accepts Catholic doctrine as certain truth. He decides to pass up the opportunity and wait for a better time *"When he is drunk asleep; or in his rage; Or in th' incestuous pleasure of his bed."*

It is from this scene that the name Hamlet has become synonymous with indecision. All those questions he said he needed to have answered before taking action were answered and his opportunity presented itself. It was his intellect that prevented him from fulfilling his mission and his intellectual reasoning seems sound, except for one thing. Claudius was not praying and asking for forgiveness because he is unwilling to give up what he has gained from his sin. He says, *"My words fly up, my thoughts remain below. Words without thoughts never to heaven go."* Things were not as they appeared, Claudius was not in a state of grace. Shakespeare leaves us wondering why Hamlet failed to act. Was it his intellectual reasoning that led him astray or was he just a coward? Did he care more about his own salvation than his beloved father's? These are just some of the unanswered questions that symbolize life's unanswered questions. The truth at

this point is that Claudius retains his crown and queen while Hamlet's father continues to suffer in purgatory.

THINK: Have you ever failed to complete an important task?

The next scene has Polonius in Gertrude's room awaiting Hamlet. This is the scene that got Freud so excited. The counsel urges the queen to be strict and stern with her son. *"Tell him his pranks have been too broad to bear with."* Polonius knows there is method in Hamlet's madness but he doesn't know what is going on and he's getting frustrated, as any counsel to a king would. Hearing Hamlet coming, he hides behind a tapestry in Gertrude's room. Earlier Hamlet said *"I will speak daggers to her, but use none."* His father's ghost had told him to leave *"my most seeming-virtuous queen"* alone and let heaven take care of her. But Hamlet was angry and was going to give his mother a piece of his mind. The great actor Laurence Olivier played the scene in the Freudian way but any way it is presented shows the prince seeming to be truly mad, in both the angry and insane way. Did he lose his mind by passing up his opportunity to avenge his father? Gertrude fears for her safety and cries for help. A noise comes from behind the tapestry. Assuming it is Claudius, Hamlet takes his sword and quickly plunges it into the figure behind the curtain, killing Polonius. No intellectual reasoning this time. *"O, what a rash and bloody deed is this!"* cries his mother. Hamlet responds saying it is almost as bad as to *"kill a king, and marry with his brother."* Gertrude doesn't know what he is talking about so Hamlet tells her what Claudius did. She cries *"O, speak to me no more! These words like daggers enter in mine ears. No more, sweet Hamlet!"* The ghost appears and tells Hamlet to take it easy on Gertrude, *"look, amazement on thy mother sits."* We are led to believe that Gertrude was unaware of Claudius' crime. Hamlet beseeches his mother to not sleep with Claudius again, *"Assume a virtue, if you have it not."* In other words, pretend you are virtuous even if you are not. He is willing to accept his mother's faults if she is willing to acknowledge them herself. The scene ends with the striking image of Hamlet tugging Polonius' dead body out of the room. The tragedy builds.

The following scene has Gertrude explaining to Claudius what happened. Hamlet is *"Mad as the sea and wind when both contend which is the mightier"* says the worried mother. We do not know if she is going to attempt virtue or stay with Claudius. Maybe she thinks Hamlet's story is the ravings of a lunatic, a teenager who has lost his mind. Or maybe she sees the truth in it. Gertrude provides plenty of fodder for analysts and philosophers to ponder. Was her amazement an act and was she a partner in the crime? Maybe she just married Claudius to insure political stability. Maybe she is a weak woman who was preyed upon by a slick man. Feminists have found much to dislike in the way Shakespeare presents women in the play. He presents Gertrude as either criminally manipulative or incompetently frail.

Frailty comes through more clearly in the character of Ophelia. We learned before The *Mousetrap* scene that Hamlet had sent love letters to Ophelia. She showed them to her father who repeated his admonition to stay away from the prince. Just after Hamlet's *"To be, or not to be"* soliloquy, Ophelia walks in and Hamlet is hostile towards her. Nothing like his sweetness at the play. Confused, she reminds him of his earlier *"words of so sweet breath compos'd."* Hamlet admits that *"I did love you once"* but three lines later he says *"I loved you not."* The audience doubts his sanity. You will feel the same way in coming years when a love interest turns from hot to cold more quickly than the weather. You will think they are insane and they may think the same about you. You both may be right as the teenage brain has all sorts of supercharged hormones racing around the new pathways still under construction. It is impossible that Shakespeare could have known about brain chemistry but he certainly understood humanity and interpersonal relations. This scene between Hamlet and Ophelia plays out constantly through the ages amongst teens learning about love. So don't worry when it happens to you too.

176

Towards the end of the play, Ophelia goes completely mad after learning about her father's death, singing bawdy songs and handing out symbolic flowers to various characters. We are somewhat surprised to see that Laertes has returned from France. The decisive son is not one to think about whether or not he should make the long journey home to mourn the loss of his father, he's there. He shows kindness, humility and patience in coming back but his anger will eventually emerge and prove tragic. A short while later, Gertrude announces that Ophelia had climbed out on a branch of a willow tree overhanging a river and fell in. Too frail to save herself, her clothes dragged her beneath the surface and she drowned. Already grieving from the loss of his father and now confronted with the death of his beloved sister, Laertes begins to lose his patience and becomes angrier, but nobody doubts his sanity.

Death in Denmark

With so many characters falling apart, the play has taken a dark turn, such as all of our lives do sometimes. In a graveyard we see Hamlet pondering life and death with Horatio and a couple of gravediggers. Hamlet had returned from his exile having pulled a stunt to send Rosencrantz and Guildenstern to England with orders that they be executed. Hamlet told Horatio how he forged the letter and sealed it with his father's signet ring that *"was heaven ordinant."* He displayed no moral struggle about killing his childhood friends and even attributes his ability to carry out the deed as heaven sent. At the same time, he sits in the graveyard struggling with his own mortality. Shakespeare frames this darkest scene with comedy, as the gravediggers tell jokes. It is another striking contradiction while also providing an example of genuine humanity. The gravediggers are trying to lighten Hamlet's mood with a little humor. You have probably done the same for a friend who was hurting in some way.

> **THINK: Have you ever doubted that anything good could come from your life?**

Holding the skull of a court jester from his youth, Hamlet wonders if the skulls of Alexander the Great and Caesar looked and smelled as bad. Yes, even the bodies of great people decompose like everyone else, it is their great legacies that they leave behind. Hamlet is really asking what happens to our souls after our bodies die. Alexander the Great and Caesar both led great advancements in civilization but were also both brutal warriors. Would their killing and oppression prevent such great people from gaining salvation? As Hamlet ponders fate, a funeral procession comes along, it is Ophelia's and we see a priest questioning the circumstances of her death, suspecting suicide. *"She should in ground unsanctified have lodg'd Till the last trumpet."* There is no doubt in the priest's mind about Ophelia's salvation; Laertes' anger begins to boil over.

Back at the palace, Claudius and Laertes develop a scheme to avenge Polonius' death by staging a fencing match with Hamlet. Not one to dither and overthink a situation, Laertes said he would poison one sword which would kill Hamlet with a simple scratch. Claudius says *"Let's further think of this"* and plans to also have a chalice of poisoned wine *"If he by chance escape your venom'd stuck"* This will prove to be an example where over thinking leads to disaster. Shakespeare is commenting that once a situation has been fully thought about, decisive action is preferable to further intellectual exploration. Claudius even says he will bet on Hamlet (with favorable odds) just to show everyone how much he wanted him to win. Doth protesting too much perhaps? It looks like a good bet as Hamlet takes the first couple of points. Claudius proclaims *"Our son shall win"* and offers him a drink but Hamlet defers until after the match. Gertrude is so happy about Hamlet doing well that she takes a drink, from Claudius' poisoned cup. The match progresses as Queen Gertrude quietly dies. Laertes gets a hit on Hamlet and tells the audience it is almost against his conscience, almost. Like Boone and Tecumseh and in contrast to Hamlet, Laertes is a man of action. Their swords get mixed up and Hamlet cuts him too. Both have been cut and poisoned with the "venom'd" sword. Laertes accepts his fate saying *"I am justly kill'd with mine own treachery."* He tells Hamlet what is going on and asks for his forgiveness. The decisive Laertes has decided to get his soul in order before he dies. *"The King, the King's to blame."* No more dithering, the poisoned Hamlet finally kills Claudius. Lying before his death he asks Horatio to tell his story and let Fortinbras take over the kingdom.

The contrast between Laertes and Hamlet is striking in that the one who studied in France is determined and decisive and accomplishes his goal in swift order. His life ends in tragedy because of his scheme to commit murder, his *"own treachery."* Like we saw with Tecumseh, virtue alone does not guarantee happiness, one weakness can end up defining an otherwise virtuous life. Hamlet's life ends in similar tragedy and everyone else has died too, including his sympathetic mother. It could have all been avoided if Hamlet had killed his uncle when he had the chance. Rather than take action, he thought about it. His intellect steered him wrong when he mistakenly thought Claudius was in prayer.

There is another obvious contrast between Fortinbras and Hamlet, two princes seeking to avenge their fathers' deaths. Before the graveyard scene, Hamlet came upon Fortinbras' army and asked a captain where they were headed to fight. He was told *"We go to gain a little patch of ground That hath in it no profit but the name."* We are not very sympathetic to the prince leading his army on a mission of mere pride. The captain prefaced his response saying *"Truly to speak"* but he was in fact lying. Remember truth is not always where it is said to be, especially when one *"doth protest too much."* Never having plans to travel to Poland, Fortinbras leads his army into the palace and seeing the death of the fencing scene in front of him, he claims the throne saying *"For me, with sorrow I embrace my fortune. I have some rights of memory in this kingdom Which now, to claim my vantage doth invite me."* It is hard to believe that Fortinbras is really claiming the kingdom with sorrow. The decisive Norwegian prince of few words has emerged the ultimate victor while the loquacious Danish prince who studied in Wittenberg lay dead. After hearing Horatio's story, Fortinbras orders a soldier's funeral for Hamlet who he says would have *"prov'd most royally"* if he had been given the chance to rule. That depends on what he means by *"royally."*

Conclusion:

You say you want a revolution
Well, you know
We all want to change the world
You tell me that it's evolution
Well, you know
We all want to change the world
But when you talk about destruction
Don't you know that you can count me out
Don't you know it's gonna be
All right, all right, all right

-    The Beatles

Being the biggest stars during the 1960s, The Beatles are inevitably associated with the Cultural Revolution whose effects are still rippling through society two generations later. The world got to know the four clean cut, well dressed lads from Liverpool, England when they broke upon the scene in 1960, and watched their hair grow long and their suits give way to hippie culture over their decade together as a band. Their songs extolling peace and love did not glorify the destruction of social norms that defined the era. Indeed they declared no role in destruction. Rather they speak to the enduring human nature that we all share and that you now understand so much better than before you picked up this book. The lines above from their song *Revolution* acknowledge the tumultuous times in which they were written while assuring us that *it's gonna be all right*.

In the preceding chapters, you have learned about the major societal shifts in recorded history so you know how society has always been *all right* afterwards, it is considered the progress of humanity. There is much to be desired of modern society in the wake of the Cultural Revolution but the flourishing of the individual and the inclusiveness of those previously excluded is undoubtedly an example of human evolution. The Beatles understood that species don't evolve into something worse, although they also warned about the bad side of revolutions. *But if you want money for people with minds that hate/ All I can tell is brother you have to wait* they sing later in the song. Revolutions are fueled by passions and The Beatles understood humanity enough to recognize those passions are often driven by the deadly sins that are part of us all.

Besides my family and my employer, The Beatles were the greatest influence on my life when I began my high school career. For someone raised in the seventies, it was impossible not to be influenced by them. Too young to remember the height of Beatlemania in the sixties, I grew up listening to my older brothers and sister play their records and their melodies became part of my formative years. Their songs had become bricks in the foundation of my life.

My father was a fan and bought their records for us. He saw them as more than pop stars and told me once that I should listen to John Lennon because he is my generation's Mozart. I don't know if my father associated The Beatles with the Cultural Revolution the way Mozart is associated with The Enlightenment of the 18th century. The two major societal shifts can be seen as bookends of a period that began with Nietzsche declaring freedom from religion and concluded with society questioning authority. The two intervening centuries were defined by the flourishing of the individual. The period produced great thinkers and scientists who have bequeathed you a world where you can define your destiny more than at any time in history. As long as you are diligent and patient about realizing your talents. The Beatles were certainly diligent. No one since Mozart has written as many melodies as The Beatles did, so they are bookends in that sense as well.

As much of a fan as my father was, he spent Christmas dinner one year explaining to his seven children how Lennon's hit song *Imagine* was actually a paean to communism. Aside from the beautiful melody, my father wanted us all to understand the song's message and decide for ourselves what we thought about having no possessions, no religion, and no hope for eternity. Yes, Lennon made me think. That lesson taught me that I can appreciate a work of art while not necessarily agreeing with its message. Likewise, I can admire a person without agreeing with their opinions. That important brick in my foundation has brought me friendships where I have gained greater knowledge and more fully enjoyed the wonderful gift of life.

Considering views that oppose your own will at least force you to reconsider your own positions. You should always be reconsidering your opinions because opinions often change. St. Thomas Aquinas taught that considering opposing views is how you find truth. He practiced a Socratic method of eliminating false theories until the truth becomes clear. So what was John Lennon saying with that song? He obviously wasn't a communist, he lived in one of New York City's fanciest buildings. One of the reasons why he lived in New York was because his native Great Britain taxed him too highly. Maybe he was pointing out the folly of communism. Maybe he just wanted his audience to think about it; I still do. Getting me to think like that made John Lennon influential in my life while his melodies make it more enjoyable. I'll never forget the morning of December 9, 1980, during my freshman year in high school, being awoken by my mother telling me that John Lennon was murdered last night.

THINK: Has any artist influenced your life?

Those bricks that he and Paul McCartney laid in my foundation cover so many aspects of life. Experiencing an artist expressing a sentiment that resonates with you reinforces that sentiment in your psyche. When others express something that you feel too, it may be a good sign that you are getting close to the truth. Hearing The Beatles sing about *the kind of things that money just can't buy* reinforced the truth that *Money can't buy me love*. It may have been easy for young millionaire rock stars to say they *don't care too much for money* but if you pursue life in a quest for personal fulfillment rather than a quest for money, the money will probably come anyway. Although you may feel like you have to work a *Hard Day's Night* to get it, and then give too much of it to the *Taxman*. It feels good to work hard and achieve goals you set for yourself because as we learned from Dr. Siegel, working hard to achieve goals will provide the healthy kind of satisfaction that keeps you on the right path in life.

Playing sports is one of many great ways to set and achieve goals. Striving to run a certain distance in a given time will develop into faster goals as you achieve those you set for yourself. The physical activity stimulates a myriad of neurotransmitters in your brain that give you the "runners high" and you realize collateral benefits like a better physique and healthier body and mind. Maybe you like music more than sports and want to learn to play a certain piece. Working and practicing to achieve it will provide the same natural and healthy satisfaction. Continue to set more goals and before you realize it, you will be proficient. Any hobby can provide opportunities to set goals and develop skills that align with your talents. You will feel a great sense of satisfaction when you achieve them.

Achieving goals will help you overcome all the challenges that life is going to throw at you, and there will be plenty. It is so important to build a habit of confronting and overcoming your challenges. Accepting challenge and uncertainty with an open mind will produce great knowledge for you. The alternative is to hunker down in your comfort zone with a cynical view of life. Everyone has problems and the greatest people through history had the greatest problems. They confidently rose to their occasions rather than be overwhelmed. They were confident that they could achieve their goals because they were optimistic about their abilities. Being confident and optimistic will help you find those talents that may yet to be revealed. Confronting and overcoming a problem can reveal talents that come to define your persona and ultimately your destiny. Like Lincoln's ability to use rhetoric and reason to rally a nation through a brutal war with the power of the truth that all men are created equal.

A positive open mind will also bring you into contact with people who will provide friendships at all of Aristotle's levels. Your friends will have similar goals and you will achieve them together as your friendships rise to the higher levels. Achieving goals will help you overcome self-doubt and give you the confidence to do anything, maybe even become a *Paperback Writer*. Your troubles will be manageable because you will know how to overcome obstacles. Achieving a goal is a great way to generate the healthy dopamine rush that everyone craves, so set goals for yourself and try to work on them *Eight Days a Week*.

THINK: Are you currently working to achieve any goals?

As a high school teen going through dramatic physical changes, love was usually the goal on my mind. Hearing Paul McCartney sing: *Well, my heart went "boom"/ When I crossed that room/ And I held her hand in mine* made my heart long for the same feeling and appreciate it when I finally felt that boom myself by the time I reached *just seventeen*. That euphoria would eventually turn to despair however when someone else caught her affection. You will experience that too and maybe you will feel less lonely when you hear someone else sing about finding and losing love. It helps you realize that it's part of the adolescent experience.

Losing those good times will make you long for *Yesterday* when *love was such an easy game to play*. There is a natural tendency to get trapped in your misery feeling like you *need a place to hide away*. You will stay home in your comfort zone and let your friends go on. Intuitively you know that retreating into your own loneliness does not let you escape the confusion of life. Quiet self-reflection and introspection are integral to self-knowledge but so is social interaction. The games we play against ourselves when alone can put us further behind. Pessimism can be more powerful than optimism. It can keep you cooped up inside, sulking alone. Your friends will begin to wonder where you went. Maybe they will think you no longer want to be friends. Confusion grows and you keep losing against yourself.

The confusion of life rings loudly in *Helter Skelter* with wild music accompanying John Lennon yelling *Do you, don't you want me to love you*. The song captures the tumult that love can inflict on us. Sometimes you will be sure to have found your soulmate only to learn that they found another soulmate. We can be so sure of things that turn out to be false, especially in the ephemeral realm of love. Not only teenagers get confused, *Hamlet* is a classic because the confusion of life is a constant throughout humanity. Oftentimes we do not even realize we are confused. Hamlet was sure that he saw Claudius in prayer, but he wasn't. Maybe he saw what he wanted to see, it gave him an excuse to delay his troublesome task. However if you always seek truth you will find it, and as Jesus tells us, the truth will set you free.[74] Working diligently and seizing the day will reveal all that life has to offer. So get out and live your life to its fullest. Be more like Daniel Boone and less like Hamlet. Remember Ovid, fortune favors the brave!

THINK: Are you brave?

When Paul McCartney sang that to *Act Naturally* meant to be a *fool* that's *sad and lonely*, he captured the way teens often feel. We see others in relationships or getting invited to parties and focus on those things we want rather the gifts we have. Human nature often leads us to dwell on the negative and fail to see the positive. Seeing what others have, we feel foolish about what we lack. Janis Joplin used alcohol and drugs to combat low self-esteem about her looks. She should have been optimistic and confident about the artistic talents she obviously possessed at a young age. She recognized the beat poets before they became a cultural force. She interpreted blues music to relate to a huge unaddressed female audience and built a fan base across genders and social demographics. Her obvious talents resulted in a number one hit song and international fame. She became a symbol of women's acceptance into previously male dominions, like rock & roll. There is no reason to think she would not have reached the same heights without being encumbered by her tragic habits. Those bad habits began in her teenage years when so many of us have low self-esteem about our still developing bodies and intellects. Even the prom queen and quarterback have their moments of low self-esteem. When you have yours, do not think you are alone; snap out of those *sad and lonely* feelings whenever they occur.

If you can't snap out of a funk, talk it through with a friend, ask if they ever felt the same. Ask other friends, family, mentors or school advisors. You may find that they experienced the same dark periods, or they may suggest you speak with someone more qualified. Don't let yourself be overwhelmed by the confusion of adolescence, it can lead to more serious troubles if not addressed. Take advantage of the great strides made in recent years in the science of the brain. You have resources available through school to address these very common teenage struggles. After reading this book, you know things that teens never knew before. Listen to the science and take care of your brain like you should take care of the rest of your body. Don't be too proud to think you don't have to take care of your mental health. It's another way of taking care of your instrument.

THINK: Are you taking good care of yourself?

Come Together

In *The Long and Winding Road,* Paul McCartney sings about *The wild and windy night, that the rain, washed away* to describe his efforts in vain to find love. Life will often feel *wild and windy* and sometimes all your efforts will feel like they've been *washed away.* The further you travel along that road the more problems you will face because you won't go far if you don't face your problems. Sometimes they will simply fade away, the trick is knowing which need to be confronted. If you are mixed up and not facing up to the ones you need to, your family and friends will let you know, so listen to them. They may not like some of the friends or hobbies you have chosen; if so, hear them out and think about what they say. Be like St. Thomas Aquinas and hear anyone out and think about what they say. The more you hear, the more the truth will stand out from the noise.

Sometimes we have trouble seeing the truth because the truth can be troubling. We are all haunted by our own personal troubles and The Beatles captured so much of that essence of life too. They sang about *Eleanor Rigby...Wearing the face that she keeps in a jar by the door/ Who is it for?/ All the lonely people.* That's her persona in the jar by the door. The face we all put on when we go out in public, or what we post online. The person we present ourselves to be. In this case it's not true, it sits in a jar, only to be used in public, and *Eleanor* is sad and lonely. Take the thought to the next level and the truth emerges that if you are true to yourself and keep a genuine persona, you won't be sad and lonely. That's because people will want to associate with someone who is good and true like you.

Even if you are lucky enough to not be sad and lonely, life is full of other kinds of problems too. When John Lennon's first marriage was failing, Paul McCartney sang *Hey Jude* to John's son Julian (Jude). The lyrics tell his friend's son to *take a sad song and make it better...The movement you need is on your shoulder.* That's your brain on your shoulder. Only you can control how you think and only you can *make your life a little better.* It's not easy to see past your troubles to all that is good, you have to initiate *that movement* in the way you think. Otherwise your troubles will consume you. The song ends with a repetition of *Na, na, na, na-na-na na/ Na-na-na na, hey Jude* with a few *yeah, yeah, yeah*s thrown in to signify all the noise and nonsense that confronts us as we struggle to *make it better*. It is a calling out from a loved one to snap out of your funk. Paul was acting as a mentor to Julian, he was forcing his best friend's son to confront the truth. That's what friends do, they stimulate that *movement on your shoulder.* An old friend of mine likes to say "if you are not having fun, it's your own fault."

Fun will come more naturally when you know yourself and live the seven virtues, which will protect you from the seven deadly sins. The sinful route may appear to be more fun but we have seen how it has proven to be the downfall of great people through history. We saw the rock stars who realized their talents as their lives collapsed under weak foundations built with alcohol in their teenage years. We also saw how living a virtuous life and becoming great does not guarantee happiness. Tecumseh was an admirable man who generally lived a virtuous life but his anger fueled a sorrow in his heart and prevented him from realizing his dream of a united nation of Indian tribes. Good things happen to good people but not always, sometimes bad things happen to good people and good things happen to bad people. It is one of life's mysteries that we can only hope are answered after our time on earth. Despite his sorrow, Tecumseh spoke the truth when he said to reach beyond what you think you can do and you will do more than you ever thought you could.

Tecumseh listened to that little angel on his shoulder, his conscience. It told him to quit drinking and more importantly, to reject his tribe's culture of torture. Your conscience is really your intellect. Your brain processes all that you know and have learned, the values your parents have instilled in you, all those bad experiences to avoid and good experiences to replicate. It knows what is good and tells you so. Listening to your conscience will keep you on a good path. So treat your brain well to keep your conscience clear. It will function better and more quickly reach that mature stage where the executive region performs like an executive's brain does. When you exercise your brain with intellectual activities, you generate those dopamine secretions in healthy productive ways. You will realize what Tecumseh was talking about and will almost surely do more than you ever imagined.

The Beatles wouldn't have been very influential in my life if they only sang about sadness and despair. They also captured the simple pleasures of everyday life as portrayed in *Penny Lane* where *there is a barber showing photographs/ Of every head he's had the pleasure to have known/ And all the people that come and go/ Stop and say hello.* The song captures humanity so well. We all enjoy the simple pleasantries of life. Sharing a smile with a neighbor, helping a stranger, or just enjoying a hobby with friends. Our culture doesn't highlight these simple pleasures but they are always present. We naturally want to enjoy the company of others and act in a pleasant way in order to foster a peaceful environment.

Problems arise when we don't realize we are acting unkindly. Someone reacts rudely to what they believe is rude and conflict arises, even if the original behavior was without any malice. It is why George Washington's first rule of civil behavior is so important, *Every action done in company ought to be with some sign of respect, to those that are present.* Be considerate of others and they will appreciate it. Of course, that includes looking up from our digital screens and acknowledging and enjoying those in our company. You can't foster a peaceful environment when you are not fully present in the environment. Part of knowing yourself is living your life in a conscious awareness of your behavior. How do you act and react?

Maybe your best friend gets invited somewhere without you, or falls in love leaving you *sad and lonely.* It is natural to begrudge such a friend, although not rational. Don't be envious of the good things that happen to others. Be happy for others' good fortune and yours will come too. Hang around people who have good things happening to them and you will learn how to make their success rub off on you. Being happy for the good fortune of others will strengthen your friendships and drive them to Aristotle's higher and more rare levels. Dr. Siegel says interaction with others is one of the best ways to build those dopamine highways. It is why friendships are so satisfying. It's that warm feeling The Beatles captured in *Penny Lane*. Learning about others teaches us about ourselves. It is a way to remove ourselves from ourselves in order to see ourselves. Learning about others is how we find those qualities that Confucius tells us to emulate and those unworthy traits that we want to avoid. Although he warned about choosing your friends carefully, I'm sure Confucius knew that having more true friends will bring you more opportunities for good fortune.

THINK: Do you have a lot of friends?

Always an important song for me is *With A Little Help From My Friends*, written by John and Paul but featuring George Harrison and Ringo Starr on vocals. Here are all four Beatles, friends indeed, collaborating on a song. When George asks if Ringo feels *sad* or *alone* Ringo sings *No I get by with a little help from my friends/ Mm I get high with a little help from my friends/ Mm gonna try with a little help from my friends.* So when that friend gets invited somewhere without you, get by with your other friends. As you develop your friendships think carefully about the next line. What does it mean to get *high with a little help from my friends*? If it means an artificially induced dopamine high, you should expect to crash down. Not just in the literal sense of your brain chemistry but in a figurative sense as well. You don't want to crash like those rock stars we saw. If you think about it, taking drugs is antisocial, it's an intensely selfish act. You may think you are being social but nobody else experiences your high. You'll be in your own world and we have seen how introducing alcohol and drugs into a reformulating teenage brain can burden that brain forever. The more you play now the more you will pay later. More importantly, the reverse is also true that paying now will let you to play more later.

This is another reason why friendships are so important. Your best friends will encourage you to develop your best qualities. It is natural because that is what you bring to the friendship. Maybe you are funny or smart or athletic or artistic. Whatever the reasons, you are someone your friends want to be around. You want to be around your friends for reasons too, maybe just to not be *sad and lonely*. That's what it means to *get by with a little help from my friends*. The fun you have together is what it means to *get high with a little help from my friends*. Having fun with your friends stimulates dopamine secretions in your brain for a healthy high.

In the case of The Beatles, the fun those four friends had together created masterful art that appeals to generations across cultures and brought them to the highest fame anyone had ever known. They were the original modern superstars. Although they became known for experimenting with drugs, it wasn't until their later years. Perhaps not coincidentally, that was near the end of the band's time together. When they were young like you, they were devoted to having fun and making music. Which brings us to the song's most important refrain. The encouragement you give and receive in a friendship and the goals you strive to achieve is what Ringo means when he sings *Mm gonna try with a little help from my friends*.

Until now you have lived in a small orbit with friends carefully screened by your parents. High school is a much bigger world where you choose your friends, so you need to go out and proactively find them. They will be happy when you arrive because with any party, the more the merrier. Do not assume a certain group is not for you. They are probably waiting for a friend like you to join their fun, you won't know until you do. Maybe a certain group is not for you, if so you will soon find out and will not want to be a part anyway. It is no fun hanging around where you are not wanted but that does not mean you are undesirable.

On the other hand, is there a group doing something appealing but you think they are a bunch of nerds? Join them and you may be pleasantly surprised. If their activity is appealing, they probably will be too when you get to know them. Do not be so proud to think you are above anyone. True friends can be hidden in unlikely places and Aristotle can tell you there is nothing better than the love that comes from true friendship.

When we find those friends we want to be around, it is easy to become cocooned in a clique, which is a group of friends who don't mix with others. It's not that we don't like others, it's just that we become too comfortable with the friends we know best. This happens because anytime we reach out to be friends with someone we take the risk of being rejected and we are naturally afraid of rejection. For some reason this is a risk that seems to play a stronger role in teenage lives than other risks. If you find your group of friends becoming a clique, try to be the one who brings other friends into the group. Everyone will appreciate you for it.

Make sure you choose friends who share your values and live within your personal guardrails. Friends aligned with your values will create a virtuous cycle where you each push the other to reach higher goals. Those higher goals will bring you great knowledge and experiences. Friends like these won't put you in difficult situations forcing you to assess the risks of what they are doing. Guardrails are easy to talk about but often difficult to discern. Knowing yourself will enable you to build your personal guardrails that we all need to keep us on the right path. Only you decide where those guardrails lie. When friends want to do something on the other side of your guardrails, wait for them to come back. If they continue beyond where you have set those limits don't change your limits, just keep on your own path that will bring you into contact with better suited friends.

Becoming an adult means setting those personal guardrails for yourself based on your own self-knowledge. From what unique weaknesses do you need to protect yourself? Are you lazy, lustful or gluttonous? Prepare for the consequences. Are you greedy or envious? Don't expect to ever be happy. How about proud or angry? Do you think anyone would want to be friends with such a person? Do you think none of those apply to you? Then you lack self-knowledge because all of them are present in all of us. The key is controlling and minimizing them.

The right friends will bring out your best qualities and help you set good habits which will establish those guardrails for your life. Setting good habits now will have a huge payoff throughout the rest of your life, just as bad habits that form in your adolescent years can have tragic consequences like all those members of the 27 Club. Those highs can reach higher than you ever imagined if you nurture your brain in a healthy way, spending time with friends, in real life, is a great way to do that.

Remember the brain research showing teenagers tend to overlook risk and over accentuate reward. Take extra time to think about the risks of what you do, knowing that your teenage brain has a natural weakness in that regard. We saw how overlooking risk can bring you new experiences, so you don't want to eliminate all risk. When I jumped off the bridge with my friends I understood the risk of getting caught and having to explain a police record for the rest of my life. I also assessed the risk of injury, especially while still under the influence of Mike's prank. However, I also knew that Mike had made the jump on several occasions as had many other friends. So I measured the risks and went ahead anyway. Now I have a story to share with you.

Your friends will want you to take many other kinds of risks with them. Think thoroughly about everything, including the risk of long term ailments. It is great to get a dopamine surge from action sports but not if you end up in a wheelchair. Let someone else strap the GoPro to their head and take the death defying leap. Choosing the right friends, knowing your abilities and understanding risk will help you push your limits safely and make you wiser as you navigate life's *Long and Winding Road*. When it comes to alcohol and drugs, you need to think about long term risks like developing an addiction that may not be recognizable until it is too late. Thinking carefully through all the risks and rewards of all the decisions you face will nurture the growth of those cognitive fibers and hasten your brain's remodeling process.

All You Need is Love

Getting out in nature is another great way to nurture your brain. There is so much going on to observe and think about. *Sit beside a mountain stream, see her waters rise/ Listen to the pretty sound of music as she flies.* I always considered myself to be *Mother Nature's Son* and The Beatles fostered that in my life too. They equate being in love with *Good Day Sunshine* and the easing of troubles with the rising sun. *Little darling, I feel that ice is slowly melting/ Little darling, it seems like years since it's been clear/ Here comes the sun, here comes the sun/ And I say it's all right.* Still one of my favorites. *"It's all right"* means that suffering is part of life and eventually ends with brighter days, so don't despair. It may take the benefit of age to realize but you will find the dark times in life will give way to brighter days. When those brighter days come you will look back on your past troubles as making you stronger and everything will be *"all right." Here Comes the Sun* is one of The Beatles' more spiritual songs, especially for New Age thinkers like George Harrison who wrote it.

In the more traditional spiritual vein is Paul McCartney singing *When I find myself in times of trouble/ Mother Mary comes to me/ speaking words of wisdom/ Let it be.* The song speaks of the calming effects of prayer and faith. We all have our *times of trouble* and how we handle them defines us. Are we cool under pressure or do we break down? The *wisdom* he sings about is the confidence that comes with faith. Faith that we have special talents and abilities that we can use to overcome our troubles. Washington's steadfastness set an example that inspired his troops to fight on through terrible adversity while MLK's eloquence inspired a nation to correct its wrongful ways. They were both men of faith who were confident enough to use their talents to achieve greatness. One of the constants through all the religions we examined is the belief that the diligence we bring to developing our individual talents defines our destinies as it did with those two great men. When the different points of view of all those religions reach the same conclusion, it's a good sign that you are finding truth. So be confident about the gifts you possess and develop them for the benefit of everyone you love and society at large.

As George and Paul addressed spirituality from opposite ends of the faith spectrum, John sang of a fuller sense of love, a Socratic sense where love transcends reality and represents all that is good. His timeless words tell us *there is nothing you can do that can't be done* but *you can learn how to play the game...Nothing that you can do but you can learn how to be you in time...Nowhere you can be that isn't where you're meant to be/ It's easy/ All you need is love.* The song spoke to me much more than the kind of love I was feeling for so many of the pretty girls I knew in high school. Lennon sang of love on a divine level, the lyrics echo St. John's biblical proclamation that God is Love.[75] Lennon is saying that with love all is possible, that love will lead us where we are meant to be, and that it is easy. Everything is easier when we are confident. Acting with love in our hearts gives us confidence that we are doing what's right. That's because if we truly act out of a sense of love, we will do what's right. At the height of their fame, John Lennon got in trouble for saying The Beatles were more popular than Jesus. To me, the message that *All You Need is Love* is the same as Jesus' message to love your neighbor as yourself.

THINK: What is a successful life?

The point of this book is to help you lead a successful life, and after reading it you now possess knowledge that will help you achieve that goal. So let's think about this important question as we finish. It is a much easier question than why we are here, which has philosophers still writing long books. Success is not about money, as indicative as that can be. It is not about fame, although the admiration of others can be a worthy metric. It is not about a life free of trouble and pain, because we know there is no such thing. It is about how we feel about our individual lives. Of course that means we need to "Know Thyself." We need to be aware of those talents we possess that can define our destiny and the weaknesses that can prevent us from fully realizing it. We need to develop our talents and overcome our weaknesses if we are to leave a proud legacy when we depart the earth.

Knowing yourself and developing your talents will put you on track for a successful life, but there is more to it. Remember what Lennon said, with love in your heart, everything is easy. Jesus said to love your neighbor as yourself and a natural place to begin is at home. It is so important to have good relationships with those who naturally love you. In a loving environment, they will help you find your talents, and won't be shy about informing you about weaknesses too. They will make it easier for you to know yourself. So be respectful of everyone in your family, and loving towards them. Love them with all their faults because they love you despite yours.

It continues in school. A loving person will naturally attract friends because people like being around good people. So don't get cocooned in a clique, get out and always meet new people, don't worry about rejection. Remember to "be not afraid!" Get out of your lazy comfort zone and roll through life cherishing it like the great gift that it is. Cherish your family and friends like the great gifts that they are. Develop and build those relationships the way you develop your own talents. You will reach many peaks of Aristotle's hierarchy. Sharing in the joys and sorrows of those you love will lead you to live a fuller life.

So what's the answer to the question? Success is a life of loving your neighbor as yourself. A life without love is the worst life imaginable so the more love in your life, the easier it will be. The Beatles summed it up beautifully in 1970 with their final words recorded as a band when they sang *"And in the end, the love you take is equal to the love you make."*

Acknowledgements:

What business does an investment advisor and commercial real estate salesman have writing a self-help book for teens? It's unlikely anyone would ever want to read it. Through the long process marked by constant self-doubt, I was sustained by the love and encouragement of so many family and friends. To my lovely wife Irene, thank you for tolerating the diversion from my profitable enterprises to pursue this long shot endeavor; if nothing else for the benefit of our three wonderful sons who you have nurtured into such excellent scholars. We all know those regular A's would not be on their report cards without your devotion to their studies and development. Nor would they be the exceptional kids for whom this book is written.

To my mother, Cathy Hickey, thank you so much for all the encouragement and support throughout the entire process, I couldn't have done it without you. Your mastery of Catechism kept the book on the right path when delving into its many Catholic subjects. I was also sustained by the strength that comes from faith, which is a lesson you have demonstrated throughout my life. The hardest time to get the book going was early in the process when I had a concept but little else. A friend with insight and knowledge of the publishing industry, as well as a parent of exceptional teens herself, encouraged me to keep going. Thank you Aimee Bell for all those discussions and reading those raw early manuscripts. Our friendship from our days at the College of the Holy Cross makes you the first Jesuit inspiration for this book. Also in that category, including parenting exceptional teens, is Peter Malia, the kind of friend that others aspire to be like. Thank you for reading the early version and making so many important editorial suggestions. The book had some glaring shortcomings before you put it back on the right path. From my high school days, my friend Liam Joyce helped me with the perspective of a high school principal who has devoted his life to the development of exceptional teens. Although we didn't attend Fordham Prep at the same time, Gregory Clancy is also owed a debt of gratitude for sharing his perceptions and copious notes of early versions. I hope his exceptional boys can also benefit from reading the book like their Hickey friends.

With so many "people for others" helping me, I have to thank an actual Jesuit too. Fr. John Sheehan, SJ provided several areas of guidance and special encouragement from his Shakespearian expertise. His observation that the Book of Genesis got the order of creation correct is an important example of how scripture interacts with science to reveal truth. I hope I presented that clearly enough to make an impression. While not a Jesuit, Fr. Albert Audette is the truest Renaissance man that I know. The fighter pilot, husband, father, grandfather, priest, author, conductor, cook and counselor also provided important feedback that resulted in a significant edit. That feedback was independently seconded by my sister Mary Gail Barry, confirming the truth that I needed to improve a certain aspect of the book. I received encouragement from many other friends and family members who were kind enough to read the book and share some thoughts. Thank you to everyone who took the time to read it and offer words of encouragement.

This book was little more than an idea and a bunch of notes assembled into a cumbersome manuscript until Natasha Reilly-Moynihan contributed her considerable editorial talents to the project. The mother of an exceptional early teen, with another close behind, brought a keen sense of where the book was reaching its audience and where it failed. Natasha "Not Good Enough," as I affectionately think of her, didn't let me move on until we had achieved our goal of engaging the reader in every section. If my stories made you think, it is because Natasha worked so hard to reach that goal. Thank you Natasha for turning this into a product that I can be proud of. The book wasn't finished though until another Jesuit alumnus added his talents. Mark Mulligan was always able to grasp what I was presenting and supplement it with his captivating illustrations. Thank you Mark for creating that important dimension to the book.

Nothing makes me more proud than my beloved sons and it may have been fortuitous that I missed my goal of publishing before my eldest Peter graduated 8th grade during 2020's pandemic. With some final pre-publication edits, he provided important feedback to where Natasha and I had succeeded in reaching him. Being such an excellent student, he even pointed out some grammatical corrections. Peter, you are a fine young man on a wonderful path in life, I hope the book helps you navigate the way.

Finally, my heartfelt thanks go to you for reading this far. If you are an exceptional early teen, I hope the stories resonate in your thoughts and reflections, and I hope you never stop thinking and reflecting. If you are a parent, I hope you have exceptional early teens who might enjoy it. If you enjoy my writing, I hope you visit www.AClassicPath.com for more.

Thank you.

* * * * *

If you enjoyed the book, the kindest compliment would be to leave a brief review at your favorite online book retailer.

Thanks again!

Endnotes:

[1] Genesis 22:10

[2] Plato, *Apology*, Section 20e

[3] Plato, *Apology*, Section 21d

[4] Matthew 22:21

[5] Nietzsche, Friedrich, *Twilight of the Idols,* "Maxims and Arrows" section

[6] https://www.pewforum.org/2017/04/05/the-changing-global-religious-landscape/pf_17-04-05_projectionsupdate_grl310px/

[7] Locke, John, *Some Thoughts Concerning Education,* Section 1

[8] CentersforDisease Control and Prevention, *National Center for Health Statistics,*2018

[9] Siegel, Daniel J., *Brainstorm: The Power and Purpose of the Teenage Brain,* Penguin Group, 2013, p. 81.

[10] Siegel, p. 69.

[11] David Dobbs, "Teenage Brains," Nationalgeographic.com, October 2011

[12] Ibid

[13] Ibid

[14] https://www.dosomething.org/facts/11-facts-about-teen-driving

[15] Weigel, George, *Witness To Hope*, Harper Collins, 1999, p. 336

[16] Tannahill, Reay, *Sex In History,* Stein and Day, 1980, p. 277

[17] Museum of Sex, *The Eve of Porn: Linda Lovelace, exhibit,* 2014

[18] Ibid

[19] Ibid

[20] Kant, Emanuel, *Treatise on Law,* Rechtslehre, 1797, Section 24, p. 87-88

[21] Wojtyla, Karol, *Love & Responsibility,* Ignatius Press, 1981, p. 55

[22] Weigel, p. 342

[23] Siegel, P. 67

[24] Siegel, p. 106

[25] Faupel, Charles E and Greg S Weaver and Jay Corzine,*The Sociology of American Drug Use, Third Edition,* Oxford University Press, 2014, p. 32

[26] Goldberg, Raymond, *Drugs Across the Spectrum, Seventh Edition,* Wadsworth Inc., 2014 p. 10

[27] Ibid

[28] Faupel, et al, p. 34

[29] Faupel, et al, p. 39

[30] Hoffman, Albert, *LSD – My Problem Child,* McGraw-Hill, 1980, p. 15

[31] Guralnick, Peter and Jorgensen, Ernst, *Elvis Day by Day: The Definitive Record of His Life and Music,* Ballantine, 1999, p. 73

[32] Marcus, Greil, *Elvis Presley: The Ed Sullivan Shows,* DVD Booklet

[33] Keogh, Pamela Clarke, *Elvis Presley: The Man, The Life, The Legend,* Simon & Schuster, 2004, p. 90

[34] Siegel, p. 68

[35] Siegel, p. 85

[36] Siegel, p. 86

[37] Siegel, p. 88

[38] Siegel, p. 82

[39] Siegel, p. 77

[40] Siegel, p. 267

[41] Siegel, p. 98

[42] Siegel, p. 262

[43] Amburn, Ellis, *Pearl, The Obsessions and Passions of Janis Joplin,* Grand Central Publishing, 1992, p. 29

[44] Amburn, p. 7

[45] Ibid

[46] Sounes, Howard, *27: A History of the 27 Club through the lives of Brian Jones, Jimi Hendrix, Janis Joplin, Jim Morrison, Kurt Cobain, and Amy Winehouse,* De Capo Press, 2013, p.115

[47] Amburn, p. 31

[48] Sounes, p. 198

[49] Amburn, p. 306

[50] Sounes, p. 12

[51] Faupel, et al, p. 243

[52] Siegel, P 71

[53] Siegel, p. 269

[54] Bakeless, John, *Daniel Boone, 1st Edition*, W. Morrow and Company, 1939, p. 81

[55] Eckert,AllanW.,*A Sorrow InOur Heart TheLifeof Tecumseh,*BantamBooks,1992,p.86

[56] Bakeless, p. 157

[57] Bakeless, p. 127

[58] Bakeless, p. 150

[59] Bakeless, p. 166

[60] Bakeless, p. 179

[61] Eckert, Allan W., *That Dark and Bloody River, Chronicles of the Ohio River Valley,* Bantam Books, 1996, p. 177

[62] Eckert, Allan W., *A Sorrow In Our Heart The Life of Tecumseh,* p. 211
[63] Ibid, p. 212
[64] Bakeless, p. 245
[65] Ibid, p. 225
[66] Ibid, p. 231
[67] Ibid, p. 259
[68] Ibid, p. 260
[69] Ibid, p. 261
[70] Ibid, p. 267
[71] Ibid, p. 318
[72] Ibid, p. 550
[73] Ibid, p. 677
[74] John 8:32
[75] 1 John 4:8

Index:

Made in the USA
Middletown, DE
11 March 2021